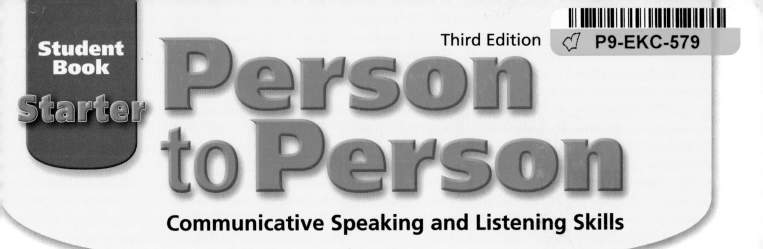

Student Book

Starter

Third Edition

P9-EKC-579

Person to Person

Communicative Speaking and Listening Skills

Jack C. Richards

OXFORD

UNIVERSITY PRESS

OXFORD
UNIVERSITY PRESS

198 Madison Avenue
New York, NY 10016 USA

Great Clarendon Street, Oxford OX2 6DP UK

Oxford University Press is a department of the University of Oxford.
It furthers the University's objective of excellence in research, scholarship,
and education by publishing worldwide in

Oxford New York

Auckland Cape Town Dar es Salaam Hong Kong Karachi
Kuala Lumpur Madrid Melbourne Mexico City Nairobi
New Delhi Shanghai Taipei Toronto

With offices in

Argentina Austria Brazil Chile Czech Republic France Greece
Guatemala Hungary Italy Japan Poland Portugal Singapore
South Korea Switzerland Thailand Turkey Ukraine Vietnam

OXFORD and OXFORD ENGLISH are registered trademarks of
Oxford University Press

© Oxford University Press 2006

Database right Oxford University Press (maker)

Library of Congress Cataloging-in-Publication Data

Richards, Jack C.
 Person to person: communicative speaking and listening skills: starter
student book /
Jack C. Richards—1st ed.
  p. cm.
ISBN 978 0 19 430210 4 (Student book)
ISBN 978 0 19 430209 8 (Student book with CD)
 1. English language—Textbooks for foreign speakers. 2. English language—
Spoken English—Problems, exercises, etc. 3. Oral communication—Problems,
exercises, etc. 4. Listening—Problems, exercises, etc. I. Title

PE1128.R463 2005
428.3'4—dc22   2005040534

Executive Publisher: Nancy Leonhardt
Senior Acquisitions Editor: Chris Balderston
Senior Editor: Patricia O'Neill
Art Director: Maj-Britt Hagsted
Senior Designer: Michael Steinhofer
Art Editor: Elizabeth Blomster
Production Manager: Shanta Persaud
Production Controller: Eve Wong

ISBN 978 0 19 430210 4 (Student Book)
ISBN 978 0 19 430209 8 (Student Book with CD)

Printed in Hong Kong.

Printing (last digit): 10 9 8 7

ACKNOWLEDGMENTS

Consider This sections written by Lewis Lansford

Illustrations by: Gary Antonetti pp. 81, 83(top map), 85; Barbara Bastian pp. 69,
82(buildings), 86(top map),104, 110; Kathy Baxendale pp.27, 34(spots),
37(watches), 43, 63, 91; Chris Costello pp.13, 29, 33; Martha Gavin pp. 3(four
people), 35, 93, 109; Neil Gower pp. 82(map), 86(bottom map), 87, 112; Mike
Hortens pp. 39, 45, 77, 103; Rob Kemp pp.42, 51, 72, 83(blank map), 97; Eric
Larsen pp. 15(room), 95(3 items top); Arnie Levin pp. 10, 13(spots bottom), 36, 38,
52; Colin Mier pp. 15(spots), 16, 34(bottom spots), 37(clocks top), 95(items
bottom); Karen Minot pp. 21, 37(clocks bottom), 61(chart), 68; Sandy Nichols pp.
3(two people), 12, 31, 56, 71 ,90; Geo Parkin pp. 7, 11(two people), 17, 30,
61(weekend activities top), 98, 107

Cover photograph by: Dennis Kitchen Studio

Location and studio photography by: Dennis Kitchen Studio pp. 2, 6, 10, 14, 18, 22,
28, 32, 36, 40, 44, 48, 54, 58, 62, 66, 70, 74, 80, 84, 88, 92, 96, 100

We would like to thank the following for their permission to reproduce photographs:
Melanie Acevedo p.67(noodles); Alamy: Anthony Blake Photo Library p.64(cola);
BananaStock pp.25(male teacher with class), 45(Chinese female); Matt Bowman
p.67(iced tea); David Brabyn p.94(Times Square); Brand X Pictures pp.25(rock
musician), 64(peppers), 94(TV); Buccina Studios p.23(2 daughters/2 sons);
Burke/Triolo Productions pp.64(lamb dish), 67(soup), 89(laptop); CheapShots
p.64(cheese); Renee Comet p.67(Bolivian breakfast); Comstock Images
p.94(iron); Comstoc Images/Almay p.80 (coffee); CORBIS: George B. Diebold
p.89(DVD player); Digital Vision pp.57, 88(international currency); Ross Durant
p.67(sushi); Don Farrall p.89(binoculars); Foodpix: Gentl & Hyers p.64(soy milk);
Gettyimages: Andersen/Ross p.25(female dentist); Dennis Gottlieb
p.64(brownies); Steve Hamblin p.64(coffee); The Imagebank p.54(multi-tasking);
Ingram Publishing p.64(seafood); Dennis MacDonald p.25(female tennis player);
Ryan McVay pp.2(Hispanic female), 89(cell phone), 89(calculator); Steven Mark
Needham p.64(yogurt); Photodisc Collection p.89(bicycle); Photodisc Green
p.67(milk shake); Photodisc Red p.44(people on computer); Donata Pizzi
p.70(young performer); Punchstock: Corbis p.94(coffeemaker); John A Rizzo
p.64(pizza); Royalty-Free p.94(telephone); Michael Steinhofer/OUP p.89(digital
camera), 89(dictionary); Stockdisc p.94(radio); Superstock p.67(ice cream
sundae); Thinkstock p.45(Caucasian male); Arthur Tilley p.23(3 sons); Joe
Vaughn p.45(African American male); Jim Wileman p.28(student surfing web);
Nick Wolcott p.18(snowboarding); Elizabeth Young p.45(Japanese female)

Special thanks to: City University of New York Graduate Center, The New York
Public Library Science, Industry and Business Library

*The publishers would also like to thank the following for their help in developing the new
edition:* Laura MacGregor, Tokyo, Japan; Su-Wei Wang, Taiwan, and Max
Wollerton, Tokyo, Japan.

*The publishers would like to thank the following OUP staff for their support and
assistance:* Satoko Shimoyama and Ted Yoshioka.

Welcome to *Person to Person*. Let's take a look at the sections of the units.

Conversations   The two conversations present examples of the language you will be studying. You can listen to them on the CD in class or at home.

Give It a Try   This section teaches the language points from the conversations. You will focus on each one separately and then practice them with a partner.

Listen to This   The listening section gives you real-life listening tasks that help you review your understanding of the language from the unit. You answer questions or complete charts about the listening.

Let's Talk   These are pair- or group-work activities that ask you to expand on what you have learned. You can use both the language you have learned and your imagination.

Consider This   "Consider This" presents some interesting facts on a cultural topic related to the theme of the unit. You can use these facts as an introduction to the unit.

Pronunciation Focus   A pronunciation point related to the language from the unit comes after Conversation 2. This helps you to practice the language in the unit in a more natural way.

Person to Person   These pages present a problem based on the language from the unit. You and a partner will work together to solve the problem, using the language you have learned, as well as your own ideas and opinions.

In addition to the language presented in each unit, here are some expressions that will be very useful to you—both inside and outside of class.

1. Please say that again.
2. I'm sorry. I don't understand.
3. Please speak more slowly.
4. How do you say _____ in English?
5. What does _____ mean?
6. I don't know.
7. May I ask a question?
8. How do you spell _____?

I hope you find that learning to speak and understand English is easier than you think. Good luck!

Contents

What are some common men's names in English? What are some common women's names?

CONSIDER THIS

"My name is …

Mariana Arrieta Colindres Barandiarán Berruguete Torrelles Dopereiro Castañeda González de Ayala. Please call me Mari." Spanish names can include up to eight family names. They come from both of your parents, your grandparents, and so on.

- How many names do you have?
- Where do they come from?

Class CD 1, Track 2

Bob:	Good afternoon.
Eun-mi:	Good afternoon.
Bob:	I'm your instructor today. My name's Robert Simpson. But please call me Bob.
Eun-mi:	Hi, Bob.
Bob:	And what's your name?
Eun-mi:	I'm Eun-mi.
Bob:	Great. And how are you today?
Eun-mi:	Fine, thanks.
Bob:	Terrific! So let's get started. Are you ready?
Eun-mi:	Yeah, let's go!

Student CD, Track 2

1. Introducing yourself

What's your name?	My name's Robert. But please call me Bob. I'm Robert.
What's your first / last name?	My first name is Robert. My last name is Simpson.

PRACTICE 1

 Class CD 1 Track 3

Listen to the example. Introduce yourself to your partner. Reverse roles.

PRACTICE 2

Class CD 1 Track 4

Listen to the example. Work in groups. Say your name. Switch roles.

My name is Tracy Park.
My first name is Tracy.
My last name is Park.
Please call me Tracy.

2. Greeting people

Informally		
Hi, Bob.	Hi, Eun-mi.	
How are you today? How are things?	Fine, thanks. Pretty good, thanks. Good, thanks. Terrific! Great.	How are you?
More formally		
Hello.	Hello, Mr. Stevens.	
Good morning.	Good morning, (ma'am).	
Good afternoon.	Good afternoon.	
Good evening.	Good evening, (sir).	

PRACTICE 1

Class CD 1
Track 5

Listen to the examples. Then practice greeting your partner informally. Reverse roles.

PRACTICE 2

Write your first name on a card (for example, *Jin-a*). On the back of the card write your last name with *Mr.*, *Ms.*, *Mrs.*, or *Miss* (for example, *Ms. Lee*).

Work in groups. Show your partners the back of your card. Practice greeting people formally. Then go around the group again. This time, hold up the front of your card. Practice greeting people informally.

3. Saying good-bye

Informally		More formally	
Bye-bye. See you later. Have a nice day.	Bye. See you. You too.	Good-bye.	Good-bye.

PRACTICE

Class CD 1
Track 6

Listen to the examples. Then practice saying good-bye to your partner. Reverse roles.

LISTEN TO THIS

Class CD 1
Track 7

Part 1 Listen to four conversations. Are the people friends, or are they meeting for the first time? Check (✔) the correct column.

Part 2 Listen again and check (✔) how each conversation ends.

	First time	Friends	How did it end?	
1			___ Have a nice day.	___ Have a nice evening.
2			___ Good-bye	___ Bye-bye.
3			___ See you again.	___ See you tomorrow.
4			___ See you later.	___ See you soon.

Part 3 In which conversation did the people know each other the best? The least? Explain your answer to a partner.

LET'S TALK

Part 1 Look at the chart below. Answer the questions, and write your information in the chart.

		You	1	2	3
1	Do you know the teacher's first name?				
2	Do you know the teacher's last name?				
3	Do you have a common first name?				
4	Do you and a classmate have the same first name?				
5	Do you and a classmate have the same last name?				

Part 2 Work in groups. Introduce yourself and then ask the questions above. Fill in the chart for each person in your group.

A: Do you know the teacher's first name?
B: No, I don't. / Yes, it's... Do you know the teacher's last name?
C: No, I don't. / Yes, it's... Do you have a common first name?
A: No, I don't. / Yes, it's... Do you...

Conversation 2
Do you want to meet him?

Where do you go to meet friends? What do you and your friends talk about?

Class CD 1, Track 8

Nishi:	Who's that guy?
Eun-mi:	That's Tony.
Nishi:	Who's he?
Eun-mi:	Oh, he's in my aerobics class.
Nishi:	He's really cute.
Eun-mi:	Yeah. Do you want to meet him?
Nishi:	You bet I do!
Eun-mi:	Tony, this is my friend Nishi.
Tony:	Hi, Nishi. Nice to meet you.
Nishi:	Hello. Nice to meet you, too.

Student CD, Track 3

Class CD 1, Track 9
Pronunciation Focus

Listen to the word *to* in these sentences.

Do you want to meet him?
Nice to meet you.

Listen to the conversation again and notice the pronunciation of *to*

1. Finding out about people

Who's that (guy)?	That's | Tony.
	Nishi.
Who's he?	He's in my aerobics class.
Who's she?	She's my friend.
Is his name Tony?	Yes, it is.
	No, it's Bob.
Is her name Maria?	Yes, it is.
	No, it's Teresa.

PRACTICE 1

Class CD 1
Track 10

Listen to the example. Look at the picture for 10 seconds. Then cover the names. Work with a partner. Ask questions to find out how many names you remember. Reverse roles.

Tony	Tina	Tim	Jason	Sunny
Yi-lin	Danny	Nishi	Yumi	Amy

Use These Words

I think he's / she's…
Is his / her name…?
I don't know.
I don't remember.

PRACTICE 2

Can you remember your classmates' names? Ask your partner questions. Reverse roles.

2. Introducing people

Informally	More formally
A: Tony, this is my friend, Nishi.	A: Tom, I'd like you to meet Bob.
B: Hi, Nishi. Nice to meet you.	B: How do you do?
C: Hi. Nice to meet you, too.	C: How do you do?

PRACTICE 1

Class CD 1 Track 11

Listen to the example. Work in groups of three. Introduce your friend Marie to these people. Switch roles.

1. to a classmate, Ricardo
2. to your teacher, Mr. Tanaka
3. to your sister, Alisa
4. to your neighbor, Mrs. Lee.

PRACTICE 2

Work in groups. Introduce one person in the group to the others. Switch roles.

LISTEN TO THIS

Class CD 1 Track 12

Part 1 Listen to Phillip introducing the people below to his friend Maya. Does Phillip introduce each person formally or informally? Check (✓) the correct column.

Part 2 Listen again and check (✓) the correct information about each person.

		Formal	Informal	A neighbor	A friend	A classmate	A teacher
1	Johnny						
2	Sandra						
3	Mr. Okano						
4	Ms. Ford						

Part 3 Talk about the conversations with a partner. Which was the most formal? Which was the most informal?

(Students A and B look at this page. Students C and D look at page 106.)

Part 1 Student A, introduce yourself to Student B. Write your information below. Reverse roles.

Student A

Mr./Ms./Mrs./Miss
First name: _____
Last name: _____

Student B

Mr./Ms./Mrs./Miss
First name: _____
Last name: _____

Part 2 Work in groups. Introduce your partner to the other people in your group. Switch roles. Write their information below.

Student C

Mr./Ms./Mrs./Miss
First name: _____
Last name: _____

Student D

Mr./Ms./Mrs./Miss
First name: _____
Last name: _____

Now Try This

Get together with a different pair of students. Introduce your partner and ask about your classmates.

Conversation 1
Are these your keys?

Do you have a cell phone?
Do you like using it?

Class CD 1, Track 13

Emily: What's that?
Akemi: It's my new cell phone.
Emily: Wow! It's really small.
Akemi: Yeah. And listen.
Emily: That's neat. And I like your sunglasses. They're cool.
Akemi: Thanks.
Emily: By the way, are these your keys?
Akemi: Oh, yes. They are mine. Thanks. Sorry, I leave my things everywhere!
Emily: I know. Here's your notebook.

Student CD, Track 4

GIVE IT A TRY

1. Identifying things (1)

What's	that?	It's my cell phone.
	this?	It's a watch.

What are	these?	They're earrings.
	those?	

PRACTICE

Class CD 1
Track 14

Listen to the example. Work with a partner and ask about these things in the picture.

sneakers	watch
backpack	cap
sunglasses	T-shirt
earrings	cell phone
socks	keys
pants	shoes

2. Identifying things (2)

Are these your keys?	Yes, they are.
Whose is this?	This is | Paul's watch.
	It's
Whose watch is this?	It's Paul's.
Whose are these?	These are | Karen's earrings.
	They're
Whose earrings are these?	They're Karen's.

PRACTICE 1

Class CD 1
Track 15

Listen to the example. Whose are they, Paul's or Karen's? Cover the picture above and ask questions about these items. Reverse roles.

A: Whose earrings are these?
B: They're Karen's.

Work in groups. Each student puts four items on the desk. How many can you correctly identify in 10 seconds? Take turns.

A: These are Keiko's sunglasses. This is David's pen. And I think this is Alicia's cell phone.

3. Complimenting people

I like your sunglasses.	They're They are	cool / nice / fun / different.
I like your bag.	It's It is	fabulous / interesting / nice.
That's a nice T-shirt.	That's	neat.
Those are nice sneakers.	They're	

**Class CD 1
Track 16**

Listen to the example. Move around the class. Greet classmates and compliment them on something.

A: Hi, Jim.
B: Hi, Kumiko.
A: How are things?
B: Pretty good, thanks.
A: Oh, I like your T-shirt. It's cool.
B: Thanks. And that's a nice watch.
A: Thanks. Well, see you later.
B: Bye.

🎯 **Use These Words**	
pretty	cool
beautiful	nice
fun	different
awesome	fabulous
gorgeous	interesting

LISTEN TO THIS

Class CD 1
Track 17

Part 1 Listen to Amanda and Suzie talking. Where are they?

___ at a clothing store ___ at the laundromat ___ at work

Part 2 Whose clothes are these? Listen again and write A for Amanda and S for Suzie.

___ socks   ___ T-shirt   ___ top   ___ jacket

___ shorts   ___ scarf   ___ dress   ___ jeans

Part 3 Talk about the clothing items above. Whose are they?

A: Whose are the socks?
B: They're Suzie's.

LET'S TALK

Part 1 Do you know what these things are? Work with a partner and name as many as you can.

A: What's this?
B: I think it's a… / I'm not sure.

Part 2 Work with another pair. Ask questions about whose these things are. Reverse roles.

A: Whose is it?
B: It's…

Mai   Hassan

Part 3 How many of these things do you have? Talk about them with a partner.

Unit 2 **13**

Conversation 2
Where are they?

Do you sometimes forget where things are? What things do you often misplace?

Class CD 1, Track 18

Akemi: Oh, I'm late again. Where are my car keys?
Taro: Are they in the drawer?
Akemi: No, they're not.
Taro: Oh, I know. They're in the bedroom, on the dresser.
Akemi: Great. Now where is my bag?
Taro: There, on the sofa next to the pillow.
Akemi: Good. Oh, but where are my glasses?
Taro: You're wearing them!
Akemi: You're right!

Student CD, Track 5

Class CD 1, Track 19
Pronunciation Focus

Listen to how the final -s is pronounced in these plurals.

[s]	[z]	[iz]
books	keys	glasses

Listen to the conversation again and notice the pronunciation of the plurals.

1. Describing where things are

Where are	my keys?	They're	in the bedroom.
	they?	They are	on the dresser.
Where's	my book?	It's	next to the sofa.
Where is	it?		under the chair.

in the drawer   *on* the table   *under* the chair

next to the TV   *in front of* the bag   *behind* the bag

PRACTICE 1

Class CD 1
Track 20

Listen to the example. Ask your partner questions about where these things are in the picture. Reverse roles.

| briefcase | keys | cap | T-shirt | watch |
| cell phone | earrings | laptop | jeans | glasses |

PRACTICE 2

Ask your partner where five other things are in the room. Reverse roles.

2. Asking where things are

Is the newspaper on the table?	Yes, it is. No, it isn't. It's on the floor.
Are the magazines on the sofa?	Yes, they are. No, they aren't. They're on the table.

PRACTICE 1

Class CD 1
Track 21

Listen to the example. Ask your partner questions about these things.
Reverse roles.

magazines
sunglasses
newspaper
camera
TV
shoes
books
remote control

PRACTICE 2

Ask your partner questions about things in the classroom. Reverse roles.

Example: Is the TV on the wall?

LISTEN TO THIS

Class CD 1
Track 22

Part 1 Listen to two people talking. Check (✔) the objects they are looking for.

___ cell phone   ___ camera   ___ TV   ___ bookshelf
___ sunglasses   ___ shoes   ___ briefcase   ___ wallet
___ tennis racket   ___ remote control   ___ magazines   ___ watch

Part 2 Listen again. Write where these things are in the room.

	Item	Location		Item	Location
1	cell phone		3	shoes	
2	camera		4	briefcase	

Part 3 Listen again. What things are in these places?

	Location	Item
1	next to the TV	
2	behind the door	
3	in the drawer	

(Student A looks at this page. Student B looks at page 107.)

...ings in the picture. Compare your picture with your
...v many differences can you find?

...era in your picture?

...ifferent partner and compare your differences.

...differences. In my picture,
...a is on the table. In my partner's
...e camera is…

Conversation 1
How old are you?

What sports do you enjoy? Is the player's height or weight or age important in these sports?

CONSIDER THIS

Student clubs ...

at Sweet Home High School in Amherst, New York, include:
Canoe Club
Computer Science Club
Rock Climbing Club
Skiing/Snowboarding Club

- Which clubs would you like to join?
- Which clubs would you not want to join?

Class CD 1, Track 23

Fu-an: I think I'd like to join the sports club.
Malik: Great. Let me ask you a few questions. How old are you?
Fu-an: I'm 19.
Malik: And how tall are you?
Fu-an: I'm 180 cm.
Malik: OK. One more thing. How much do you weigh?
Fu-an: I weigh 70 kilos.
Malik: And what kinds of sports are you interested in?
Fu-an: I like all team sports, and I also like swimming.

Student CD, Track 6

1. Describing personal information

How old	are you? is he / she?		I'm 18. She's 20.
How tall	are you? is he / she?		I'm 172 centimeters tall. She's 180 cm tall.
How much	do you does he / she	weigh?	I weigh 65 kilos. He weighs 72 kilos.

PRACTICE 1

Class CD 1
Track 24

Listen to the example. Work in groups. Complete the information in the chart about people in your group.

	Name	Age	Height
1			
2			
3			
4			

PRACTICE 2

Class activity. Read the information about someone in your group. Others guess who it is.

Example: She's 21. She's 165 cm. Who is she?

2. Talking about interests (1)

Are you interested in sports?	Yes, I am. Sure. Not really.
What kind of sports are you interested in? What kind?	I like team sports I like swimming. (I'm interested in) tennis and baseball.

PRACTICE 1

Look at the list of sports below. Check (✔) the sports you are interested in.

Sports	Me	My partner	Sports	Me	My partner
baseball			skiing		
soccer			tennis		
golf			Your idea: _____		

PRACTICE 2

Class CD 1
Track 25

Listen to the example. Then ask a partner about the sports he or she is interested in. Check (✔) the answers in the chart above. Reverse roles.

Use These Words

outdoor/indoor sports
winter/summer sports
team/individual sports
badminton

3. Talking about interests (2)

Are you interested in	movies? music?		Yes, I am. Yeah. Not really.
What kind of	movies	are you interested in?	I like	comedies. horror movies.
What kind?	music		I like reggae. (I'm interested in) rock.

PRACTICE 1

Class CD 1
Track 26

Listen to the example. What are you interested in? Check (✔) the things you like in the list below. Then ask a partner. Reverse roles.

___ art   ___ clothes
___ nature   ___ reading
___ travel   ___ video games
___ food   ___ shopping

Use These Words

paintings
pottery
rivers
novels
sculptures
forests
wildlife
poetry

LISTEN TO THIS

Class CD 1
Track 27

Part 1 Listen to three conversations. What do the people want to do? Write the number of the conversation next to each activity.

___ join a sports club   ___ watch a baseball game   ___ go shopping

Part 2 Listen again. How old are they? How tall are they? Complete the chart.

	Age	Height	Sports
David			
Meena			
Sandra			

Part 3 Talk about the sports each person is interested in.

LET'S TALK

Part 1 Class survey. Look at the chart below and write your answers in the chart.

Part 2 Work in groups of four. Take turns asking your classmates about age and height, and the kinds of music, sports, and movies they are interested in. Also ask questions about your own idea.

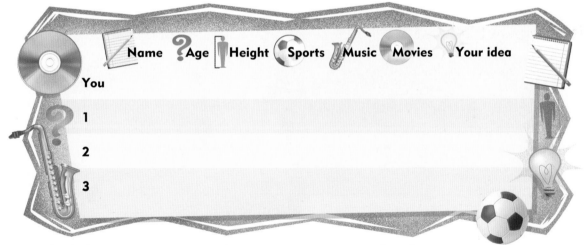

Part 3 Who has interests similar to yours? Report to the class.

Conversation 2
Tell me about your family.

Do you come from a big family? How many people are in your family?

Class CD 1, Track 28

Fu-an:	So, Eva. Tell me about your family.
Eva:	Well, I come from a medium-sized family.
Fu-an:	How many brothers and sisters do you have?
Eva:	I have one brother and one sister.
Fu-an:	How old are they?
Eva:	My sister Rosie is 12 and my brother David is 22.
Fu-an:	Oh. And what do your parents do?
Eva:	My father is an engineer and my mother is a pharmacist.
Fu-an:	How old are they?
Eva:	My mother is 44 and my father is 45.

Student CD, Track 7

Class CD 1, Track 29
Pronunciation Focus

Wh- questions usually have falling intonation. Listen to the intonation in these questions:

How many brothers and sisters do you have?
What do your parents do?
How old are they?

Listen to the conversation again and notice the intonation of the questions.

GIVE IT A TRY

1. Talking about family members

Tell me about	your Sam's	family.	I come from He comes from	a big / medium-sized / small family.

How many brothers and sisters	do you have? does he have?	I have He has	two sisters. one sister.

Do you	have any brothers and sisters?	Yes, I do. No, I don't. I'm an only child.
Does Aya		Yes, she does. No, she doesn't.

PRACTICE 1

Class CD 1
Track 30

Listen to the example. Look at these pictures of Sam's and Kendra's families. With a partner, ask and answer questions about them.

Sam's family

Kendra's family

PRACTICE 2

Talk to your partner and complete the chart about his or her family.

Partner's name	How many brothers and their ages	How many sisters and their ages

2. Asking about family members

What do your parents do?	My father is an engineer and my mother is a pharmacist. My parents are retired. My mother is a homemaker.
How old are they? / your parents?	My father / dad is 44 and my mother / mom is 42.
What are their names?	My dad's name is John, and my mother's name is Karen.

PRACTICE

Class CD 1 Track 31

Listen to the example. Complete the chart with information about your parents. Then talk to a partner and find out about his or her parents. Reverse roles.

Me	My partner
Father's name	Father's name
Age	Age
Occupation	Occupation
Mother's name	Mother's name
Age	Age
Occupation	Occupation

LISTEN TO THIS

Class CD 1 Track 32

Part 1 Michelle is a homestay student from Korea. She is talking to her host family. What topics do they talk about?

___ family size ___ occupations ___ sports ___ movies ___ music

Part 2 Listen again and complete the information.

	How many?	Ages
Brothers		
Sisters		

Part 3 What do Michelle's parents do?

	Occupation
Mother	
Father	

(Student A looks at this page. Student B looks at page 108.)

Part 1 Look at the photos of Salina and Brendan. Your partner has information about them. You will ask your partner questions about them.

Salina

Brendan

Write the questions you will ask to find out their age, height, family, and interests.

1. _____ ?   4. _____ ?
2. _____ ?   5. your idea: _____ ?
3. _____ ?

Part 2 What does Salina do? What does Brendan do? Tell your partner what you think.

Part 3 Now answer your partner's questions about Pelisa and Trent.

Pelisa
25 years old
150 centimeters
Mother: homemaker
Father: dentist
no sisters, 2 brothers
Interests: doesn't like
movies; likes golf, all music,
science and medicine

Trent
20 years old
180 centimeters
Mother: artist
Father: actor
2 sisters, no brothers
Interests: likes movies,
sports, all music,
especially rock music

Part 4 What does Pelisa do? What does Trent do?
Tell your partner what you think.

Now Try This

Imagine you are going to
interview a celebrity. Who
will you interview? What
questions will you ask?
Make a list.

Review:
Units 1–3

Class CD 1
Track 33

Part 1 Listen to two people talking. Check (✓) if the statements below are *true* or *false*.

	True	False
1. Paul is taking music lessons.	☐	☐
2. Taylor is his teacher.	☐	☐
3. Her last name is Johnson.	☐	☐
4. Robert is Paul's brother.	☐	☐
5. Robert is a friend of Taylor's.	☐	☐

Part 2 Ask your partner questions to find out if your answers are the same.

GIVE IT A TRY

Part 1 Match the phrases in **A** with suitable responses in **B**.

A	B
1. Good evening.	___ I'm Ricardo.
2. How are you doing?	___ Nice to meet you, too.
3. My name is Tony.	___ Pretty good, thanks.
4. Nice to meet you.	___ Hello.

Part 2 Now practice the conversation with a partner. Use your own names.

LISTEN TO THIS   UNIT 2

Class CD 1
Track 34

Part 1 Listen to people asking where these things are in a room. They are looking at the table. Number where each item is from 1–6.

1. the bag	—— It's in the drawer.
2. the umbrella	___ It's on the table.
3. the notebook	___ It's under the table.
4. the watch	___ It's behind the table.
5. the cell phone	___ It's next to the table.
6. the newspaper	___ It's in front of the table.

Part 2 Ask your partner questions to find out if your answers are the same.

1. Describing colors and clothing

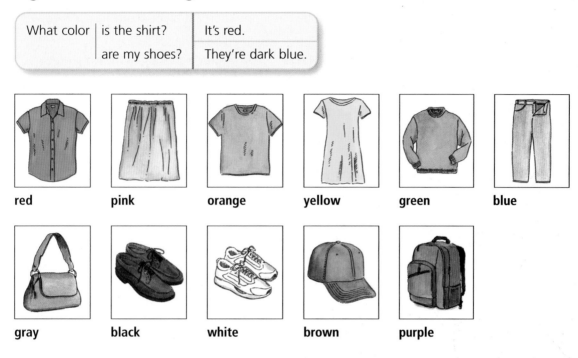

| What color | is the shirt? | It's red. |
| | are my shoes? | They're dark blue. |

red   pink   orange   yellow   green   blue

gray   black   white   brown   purple

PRACTICE 1

Class CD 1
Track 37

Listen to the example. How many different colors are you wearing today?
Write down at least four colors. Then ask your partner. Reverse roles.

A: What colors are you wearing today?
B: My shirt is red. My shoes are dark blue.

PRACTICE 2

Ask your partner questions about the color of classmates' clothes.
Reverse roles.

A: What color is Hong-yi's shirt?
B: It's yellow and red.

PRACTICE 3

Student A says a color. Student B tries to find someone in the class with
the color. Reverse roles.

A: Pink.
B: Julia has a pink purse.

Use These Words	
shirt	glasses
skirt	necklace
dress	ring
sweater	gold
coat	silver

2. Describing people

What does	he	look like?	She's tall / medium height / short.
	she		He's thin / a little heavy.
	Sandy		She has long / short / straight / curly hair.
What is	she	wearing?	She's	wearing	a red dress.
	he		He's		gray pants and a brown jacket.
Is she wearing glasses?			Yes, she is.
			No, she isn't.

PRACTICE 1

Class CD 1 Track 38

Listen to the example. Ask your partner to describe the people in the picture and say what they are wearing. Reverse roles.

A: What does Sandy look like?
B: She's medium height. She's wearing brown pants and a red shirt.

Sandy   Derek   Vickie   Sanjay

PRACTICE 2

Think of a classmate and describe him or her. Your partner asks questions and tries to guess who you are describing. Reverse roles.

A: Is she / he tall?
B: Yes, she / he is.
A: Is she / he wearing blue jeans?
B: No, she / he isn't.
A: Is it Woo-jin?
B: Yes, it is!

LISTEN TO THIS

Part 1 Listen to someone describe five people. Check (✓) the qualities you hear described.

___ height   ___ weight   ___ hair   ___ personality
___ glasses   ___ interests   ___ clothing

Part 2 Listen again and number the people you hear about.

Simon ___   Bill ___   Ted ___   Anne ___   Jolene ___   Ken ___   Maria ___

Part 3 Listen again. What is the relationship between the people you heard about? Who are the following?

1. best friends: _____
2. brothers: _____
3. brother and sister: _____

LET'S TALK

Part 1 Complete the chart about yourself.

	You	Your Partner
Colors that I like to wear		
Colors that I don't like to wear		
Clothes I usually wear to school		
Clothes I usually wear on the weekend		
Clothes I bought recently		
Clothes I want to buy		

Part 2 Talk to a partner and complete the chart with his or her information. Reverse roles.

A: What are colors that you like to wear?
B: I like…
A: What are clothes that you don't like to wear?
B: I don't like…

Conversation 2
Do you like this sweater?

How often do you shop for clothes? Where do you like to shop for clothes?

Class CD 1, Track 40

Joe:	How do you like this sweater?
Ana:	Hmm… I don't like it very much. I don't like the color.
Joe:	OK. Well, how about this one?
Ana:	Yes, it's great. How much is it?
Joe:	It's 15 dollars.
Ana:	Fifty dollars!
Joe:	No, 15.
Ana:	Fifteen. That's not bad.
Joe:	Excuse me, please. I'd like to try this on.
Clerk:	Certainly. The changing room is over there.
Joe:	Thank you.

Student CD, Track 9

Class CD 1, Track 41
Pronunciation Focus

Listen to the difference between these numbers.

thirteen	thirty
fourteen	forty
fifteen	fifty

Listen again and notice the numbers in the conversation.

1. Giving opinions

How do you like	this sweater? these shoes?	It's They're	great. nice. OK.
		I don't like it / them very much.	
		I like I don't like	the color. the style. the design.

PRACTICE 1

Class CD 1
Track 42

Listen to the example. How do you like these things? Mark them from *1* (you like them a lot) to 5 (you don't like them). Then ask your partner. Reverse roles.

shoes

shirt

dress

scarf

T-shirt

jacket

coat

glasses

PRACTICE 2

Do you have any of the items above? Which ones? What do you like about them? Tell your partner. Reverse roles.

Example: I have a scarf. I like it because it's very soft and it's bright green.

Use These Words	
bright	soft
dark	warm
colorful	comfortable
stylish	

2. Talking about prices

How much	is	it?the watch?	It's $15.$55.
	are	the shoes?	They're $45.
That's	not bad.expensive.reasonable.cheap.		

PRACTICE

Listen to the example. How much do you think these things cost? Write a price in dollars or in your own currency beside each item. Then compare with a partner.

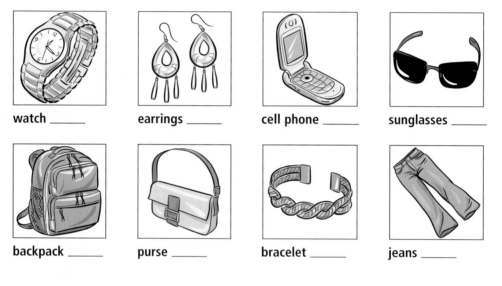

watch _____   earrings _____   cell phone _____   sunglasses _____

backpack _____   purse _____   bracelet _____   jeans _____

LISTEN TO THIS

Part 1 Jenny and Dave are shopping. How do they like the items? Listen and check (✓).

Part 2 Listen again. How much does each item cost? Write the prices.

①	②	③	④
like it a lot	like them a lot	like it a lot	like them a lot
think it's OK	think they're OK	think it's OK	think they're OK
don't like it	don't like them	don't like it	don't like them
Price:	Price:	Price:	Price:
Bought?	Bought?	Bought?	Bought?

Part 3 Did they buy the item? Write *yes* or *no*.

(Student A looks at this page. Student B looks at page 109.)

Part 1 You are going to meet a friend at a party. Look at the picture of your friend. What does he look like? What is he wearing? Make notes.

Dan

Part 2 You are at the party now, but you don't see your friend. Describe him to your partner. Your partner will tell you where he is.

Part 3 Now your partner is going to ask you about one person in the picture above. Listen to the description, and tell your partner where she is.

Now Try This

Think of unusual clothing you have seen recently (e.g., in a magazine, on television, or on the street). Describe it to your partner.

Are you an early bird (you get up early)?
Are you a night owl (you go to bed late)?

Class CD 1, Track 45

Jade:	Who are you calling?
David:	I'm calling my sister in Sydney, Australia.
Jade:	What time is it there?
David:	I'm not sure.
Jade:	Well, it's 2 P.M. here, so it's about 12 A.M. there. That's very late.
David:	No problem. My sister always goes to bed late.
Jade:	Really. What time does she go to bed?
David:	Around 2 A.M. She's a real night owl!

Student CD, Track 10

1. Telling the time

What time is it?		
It's ten o'clock.	It's five after ten.	It's ten fifteen.
	It's ten oh five.	It's a quarter after ten.
It's ten thirty.	It's ten forty.	It's ten forty-five.
	It's twenty to eleven.	It's a quarter to eleven.
It's 10 A.M.	It's 10 P.M.	

PRACTICE 1

Class CD 1 Track 46 Listen to the example. With a partner, take turns saying these times.

PRACTICE 2

Class CD 1 Track 47 Listen to the example. Take turns asking about these times.

PRACTICE 3

Look at the time in these different places. Ask your partner questions like this:

A: It's 10 A.M. in Tokyo. What time is it in New York?
B: It's 8 P.M.

New York	Paris	Athens	Bangkok	Taipei	Seoul	Tokyo	Sydney
8:00 p.m.	2:00 a.m.	3:00 a.m.	8:00 a.m.	9:00 a.m.	10:00 a.m.	10:00 a.m.	11:00 a.m.

2. Talking about routines

What time do you get up?	I usually get up at 6:30.
When do you go to bed?	At about 11:30 P.M.
What time does your sister get up?	She gets up at around 5 A.M.
When does she go to bed?	She goes to bed at around 9 P.M.

PRACTICE 1

Class CD 1
Track 48

Listen to the example. Tell your partner about your routine. Compare the times you do these things.

get up

have breakfast

leave home in the morning

get home

have supper

go to bed

PRACTICE 2

Work in groups. Compare your routines. Who are the early birds? Who are the night owls?

A: Jackie is an early bird. She gets up at 5:30 A.M.
B: Peter is a night owl. He goes to bed at 3 A.M.

LISTEN TO THIS

Class CD 1
Track 49

Part 1 Listen to four people talking about their work. Do they like their jobs? Write *yes* or *no*.

1. Chris _____   2. Kayla _____   3. Tim _____   4. Celia _____

Part 2 Listen again. When do they start work? When do they finish work? Write the answers in the chart, then compare with a partner.

	Hair stylist	Dog walker	Ticket seller	Ballet teacher
Starts:				
Finishes:				

Part 3 What hours do members of your family work? Does anyone work similar hours to one of the people above? Tell your partner.

LET'S TALK

Part 1 What are you going to do this weekend? Write in the things you plan to do.

Saturday

8:00 am _____
9:00 am _____
10:00 am _____
11:00 am _____
12:00 pm _____
1:00 pm _____
2:00 pm _____
3:00 pm _____
4:00 pm _____
5:00 pm _____
6:00 pm _____
7:00 pm _____
8:00 pm _____

Sunday

8:00 am _____
9:00 am _____
10:00 am _____
11:00 am _____
12:00 pm _____
1:00 pm _____
2:00 pm _____
3:00 pm _____
4:00 pm _____
5:00 pm _____
6:00 pm _____
7:00 pm _____
8:00 pm _____

January February March April May June July August September October November December

Part 2 Now talk to a classmate and ask questions like these.

1. When are you free on Saturday?
2. When is a good time for us to see a movie?
3. When are you free on Sunday?
4. When is a good time for us to (your idea) _____?

Use These Words

go out with friends   watch TV
study English   sleep in
go shopping   play sports
go to the library   see a movie

Conversation 2

Are you busy?

What is the busiest day in your week?
What do you do on that day?

Class CD 1, Track 50

Jade: Are you very busy this semester?
Wei-de: So-so.
Jade: What days do you have classes?
Wei-de: I have classes on Tuesday, Wednesday, and Friday.
Jade: And what do you do in your free time?
Wei-de: Well, I go to the gym on Monday and Thursday. And I play tennis on Saturday afternoon.
Jade: Wow! You must be in really good shape! And what do you do on Sunday?
Wei-de: On Sunday I sleep until noon!

Student CD, Track 11

Class CD 1, Track 51
Pronunciation Focus

Listen to the stress in these question

What days do you have classes?
What do you do on Sunday?

Listen to the conversation again a
notice the stressed words.

GIVE IT A TRY

1. Talking about the week

Weekdays	The weekend
Monday Tuesday Wednesday Thursday Friday	Saturday Sunday

PRACTICE 1

Class CD 1
Track 52

Listen to the example. Practice saying the days of the week with a partner.

PRACTICE 2

Check (✓) when you usually do these things. Then ask a partner when he or she does them. Reverse roles.

	On weekdays	On the weekend
Study English		
Go out with friends		
Play sports		
Stay in and study		
Watch TV		
Watch movies		
Sleep late		

A: When do you study English?
B: On the weekend. When do you…?

PRACTICE 3

What are two other things you do on weekdays and on the weekend? Talk to a partner and compare answers.

Example: On weekdays I play video games and I…

2. Talking about activities

What days do you have classes?		On Monday and Friday.
What do you do	on Friday nights?	I meet my friends.
	after class?	I go to a club.
Do you have classes on Friday?		Yes, I do. No, I don't.

PRACTICE 1

Complete this schedule with one thing you do each day of the week.

Monday	Tuesday	Wednesday	Thursday	Friday	Saturday	Sunday

PRACTICE 2

**Class CD 1
Track 53** Listen to the example. Compare your schedule with a partner's.

LISTEN TO THIS

**Class CD 1
Track 54** *Part 1* Paul and Hannah are trying to find a time to get together. When can they meet?

Part 2 Listen again and write the day and time that Paul is going to do these things.

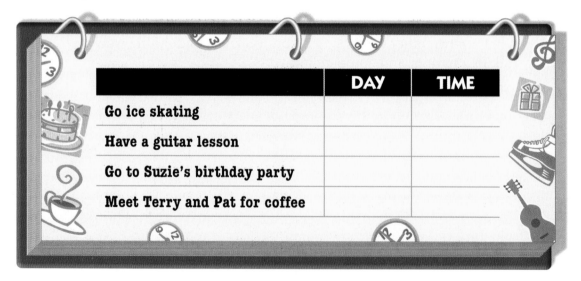

	DAY	TIME
Go ice skating		
Have a guitar lesson		
Go to Suzie's birthday party		
Meet Terry and Pat for coffee		

Part 3 Who is busier, Paul or Hannah? Whose schedule is similar to yours?

Part 1 Complete the information about yourself.

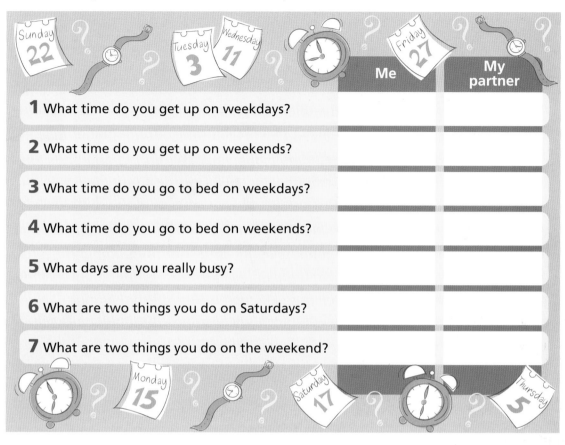

	Me	My partner
1 What time do you get up on weekdays?		
2 What time do you get up on weekends?		
3 What time do you go to bed on weekdays?		
4 What time do you go to bed on weekends?		
5 What days are you really busy?		
6 What are two things you do on Saturdays?		
7 What are two things you do on the weekend?		

Part 2 Talk to a partner and fill in the chart with your partner's information.

Part 3 Compare your answers. How similar are you and your partner?

Now Try This

How well do you know your classmates? Choose a classmate and guess his or her answers to the questions above. Then talk to the classmate and compare your information.

Conversation 1

Tell me about yourself.

What are you studying? How do you like your classes?

Class CD 1, Track 55

Lisa: So what do you do, Emi?
Emi: I'm a student. I'm studying fashion design.
Lisa: That's interesting. And where are you studying?
Emi: At City College.
Lisa: How do you like your classes there?
Emi: I love them. They're a lot of fun.
Lisa: That's great.
Emi: So what do you think of my top? It's my own design.
Lisa: It's awesome!

Student CD, Track 12

1. Talking about school

What	do you	do?	I'm a student. I go to school / college.		
	does Emi		She's She is	a college student.	
What	are you	studying?	I'm studying	majoring in	business. IT.
	is Emi		She's		fashion design.
Where	are you is Emi	studying?	I go She goes	to City College.	

PRACTICE 1

Class CD 1
Track 56

Listen to the example. Ask your partner questions about these people.
Reverse roles.

1. What does (Rod) do?
2. Where is (Tina) studying?
3. What is (Michiko) majoring in?
4. Where does (Thomas) study?

Complete the chart about yourself. Then ask a partner the questions below.
Reverse roles.

		You	Partner
1	Occupation		
2	Area of study		
3	School		

1. What do you do?   2. What are you studying?   3. Where are you studying?

2. Giving an opinion about school and study

How do you like	your classes?	I like them a lot.
	your school?	It's good.
	studying English?	It's OK.
		It's so-so.

PRACTICE 1

**Class CD 1
Track 57**

Listen to the example. Ask a partner about the things below. Reverse roles.

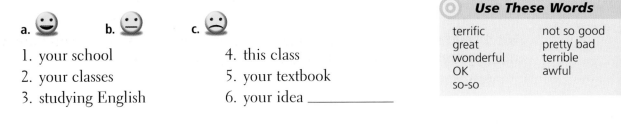

a.   b.   c.

1. your school	4. this class
2. your classes	5. your textbook
3. studying English	6. your idea _____

Use These Words

terrific	not so good
great	pretty bad
wonderful	terrible
OK	awful
so-so	

PRACTICE 2

Check (✓) your opinion about these ways of learning English. Then ask your
partner questions about them. Reverse roles.

		I like it a lot.	It's good.	It's OK.	It's so-so.
1	Studying grammar				
2	Practicing dialogs				
3	Learning vocabulary				
4	Working with a partner				
5	Working in groups				
6	Using the computer lab				
7	Listening to songs				

A: How do you like using the computer lab?
B: I like it a lot. Do you?
A: It's OK.

46   Unit 6

LISTEN TO THIS

Class CD 1
Track 58

Part 1 Listen to Martin, Rosie, and Liz talking about school. Who likes school the most? Who likes it the least?

Part 2 Listen again and check (✓) the kind of school they are studying in and their major.

	School		Major				
	Junior College	University	Liberal Arts	IT	Music	Business	Tourism
Martin							
Rosie							
Liz							

Part 3 Listen again and check (✓) how well they like their school and their major.

	School			Major		
	Like it a lot	So-so	Don't like	Like it a lot	So-so	Don't like
Martin						
Rosie						
Liz						

Part 4 Talk to your partner about Martin, Rosie, and Liz. Who do you think will change their major? Who will be most successful in school?

LET'S TALK

Part 1 Complete the chart with information about yourself. What are some subjects you are studying? How do you like them? Choose from the following: *difficult, interesting, useful, easy, OK, boring.*

Subject	My opinion

Part 2 Work in pairs. Student A asks questions, and Student B answers. Reverse roles.

A: What subjects are you studying this year?
B: I'm studying math, marketing, English, and…
A: How do you like math?
B: It's OK.
A: How about marketing?

Use These Words

history	political science
economics	biology
physics	engineering
law	medicine

Conversation 2
Tell me about your friend.

Do you spend a lot of time with your friends? What are they like?

Class CD 1, Track 59

Ali: So, who is your best friend?

Emi: I guess that's my friend Sara.

Ali: Tell me about her. What's she like?

Emi: Oh, she's great. She's very funny. And she's interesting to talk to.

Ali: Really?

Emi: Yes, she's very outgoing and talkative.

Ali: And is she easygoing?

Emi: Oh, sure. That's why I like her. The only thing is, she's forgetful at times. She's not very reliable.

Ali: Yeah?

Emi: Yes. We have an appointment, and she's late. That's Sara!

Class CD 1, Track 60
Pronunciation Focus

Listen to stressed syllables in these words.

1st syllable	2nd syllable
different	easy**go**ing
talkative	re**li**able
interesting	for**get**ful

Listen to the conversation again and notice the stressed syllables.

1. Talking about personal qualities

What's	Sarah	like?	She's fun and she's talkative.
	David		He's easygoing and outgoing.
Is she	easygoing?		Yes, she is. She's very easygoing.
	reliable?		No, she's not very reliable.

PRACTICE 1

Class CD 1
Track 61

Listen to the example. Do you think the qualities below are positive or negative? Write them in the chart below. Compare with a partner.

talkative   fun   unreliable   different   outgoing   easygoing
impatient   shy   interesting   patient   serious   reliable

Positive qualities	Negative qualities

PRACTICE 2

Work with a partner. Describe at least three qualities of one of your friends. Reverse roles.

A: I'm going to talk about my friend Tina.
B: What's she like?
A: Well, she's fun and easygoing. And she's talkative.
B: Is she reliable?
A: Yes, she is.

2. Comparing personal qualities

How similar are you and your	best friend?	We are both talkative.
	brother / sister?	She's patient, but I'm impatient at times.

PRACTICE 1

Class CD 1
Track 62

Listen to the example. Work with a partner. Talk about you and a friend, brother, or sister. Reverse roles.

A: Who is your best friend?
B: My best friend is my sister, Anna.
A: How similar are you?
B: Well, we are both talkative.
A: And how are you different?

Use These Words

polite
entertaining
reliable
outgoing
serious

PRACTICE 2

Complete this chart about you and a friend. Use the words above and on page 49. Then work with a partner and compare your information.

	Some similarities	Some differences
Me		
My friend		

LISTEN TO THIS

Class CD 1
Track 63

Part 1 Listen to Colin talking about his new roommate in the college dormitory. Check (✓) the things he likes about his roommate.

Part 2 Listen again. Mark the things he doesn't like with an **✗**.

		Likes	Dislikes			Likes	Dislikes
1	friendly			5	untidy		
2	interesting			6	lazy		
3	funny			7	forgetful		
4	good student			8	impolite		

Part 3 List the three qualities you think are most important for a roommate.

PERSON TO PERSON STUDENTS A AND B

Part 1 Read the questions. Then write your answers in the chart below.

1. What are your favorite school subjects?
2. What subjects don't you like?
3. What are some of your good qualities?
4. What are some of your not so good qualities?

Me		My partner	
Favorite school subjects	**School subjects I don't like**	**Favorite school subjects**	**School subjects he/she doesn't like**
My good qualities	**My not-so-good qualities**	**My partner's good qualities**	**My partner's not-so-good qualities**

Part 2 Work in pairs. Ask your partner the questions above and write his or her information in the chart.

Part 3 Work in groups. Tell the group about your partner. How similar are people in your group?

Now Try This

Which of the fields below best suits you? Why? List some of your personal qualities that make it a good choice for you. Compare your answers with a partner's.

- Sales and marketing
- Business
- The arts/entertainment

Review:
Units 4–6

LISTEN TO THIS UNIT 4

Class CD 1
Track 64

Part 1 Kim is meeting Bob at the airport. They have not met before. Listen to their telephone conversation and write their information in the chart.

	Height	Hair	Clothes
Bob			
Kim			

Part 2 Ask your partner questions to find out if your answers are the same.

GIVE IT A TRY

Part 1 Look at these two sisters. Compare how they look: their height, weight, what they are wearing. How many differences can you find between them?

Part 2 Work with a partner. Then discuss with others. Who has the most differences?

LISTEN TO THIS UNIT 5

Class CD 1
Track 65

Part 1 Anna and Dave are trying to find a time to meet for dinner this week. When are they doing the things below? Write A when Anna is busy, and D when Dave is busy.

		Mon.	Tues.	Wed.	Thurs.	Fri.	Sat.	Sun.
1	Have late classes							
2	Play basketball							
3	Go to the gym							
4	Have a driving lesson							
5	Have a meeting							
6	Meeting friends							

Part 2 When can they meet?

GIVE IT A TRY

Work with a partner. Student A is visiting your city and asks the questions below. Student B answers the questions. Reverse roles.

1. What time do banks open here? And what time do they close?
2. How about department stores? What are their opening and closing times?
3. What about schools? What time do classes start and finish at public schools?
4. And what time does the subway run until during the week? How about on weekends?

LISTEN TO THIS   UNIT 6

Class CD 1
Track 66

Part 1 What qualities do you think are important for the people below? Mark your answers with an ✗. Then listen to two people giving their opinions. Mark their answers with a check (✓).

	Important qualities for...	
	Roommate	**Travel companion**
1 friendly		
2 outgoing		
3 easygoing		
4 relaxed		
5 talkative		
6 responsible		
7 practical		
8 considerate		

Part 2 Do you agree with them? Ask your partner questions to find out if your answers are the same.

GIVE IT A TRY

Work with a group. What's your opinion of these subjects? Choose three words to describe them, then compare your answers with your partners'.
difficult, easy, fascinating, boring, useful, not very useful, fun, so-so, important

Subjects	Math	Computers	Literature	English
Opinions				

What's your favorite weekend activity? What *don't* you like to do on the weekend?

Activity	hours per week
attend class	16
study	15
use a computer	7
exercise	6
watch TV	5.5

- How many hours do you spend each week on these activities?
- What else do you do?

Class CD 2, Track 2

Mei-ho: What do you usually do on Saturday?

Tasha: I usually get up early and go for a run in the morning. Then I meet my friends and we have brunch together.

Mei-ho: What about in the afternoon?

Tasha: In the afternoon I often see a movie or go over to my friend's house.

Mei-ho: And do you ever play sports on the weekend?

Tasha: Yeah, sometimes I play tennis.

Mei-ho: I love tennis. Why don't we play together sometime?

Tasha: Sure. That sounds great.

Student CD Track 14

GIVE IT A TRY

1. Talking about routines (1)

> What do you usually do on Saturday morning / afternoon / evening?
>
> I usually get up early in the morning.
> In the afternoon, I often see a movie.
> In the evening, sometimes I meet friends.

0%   100%

Never   Sometimes   Usually   Always
                       Often

PRACTICE 1

Class CD 2 Track 3

Listen to the example. Do you do any of these things on Saturday? Check (✓) your answers, then ask your partner about his or her activities. Reverse roles.

	Me	My partner
Sleep in		
Play sports		
Have classes		
Play video games		
Go to the movies		
Surf the web		
Do homework		
Hang out with friends		

PRACTICE 2

Class CD 2 Track 4

Listen to the example. List other things you do at these times on Saturday. Then ask your partner what he or she does. Reverse roles.

1. in the morning: _____

2. in the afternoon: _____

PRACTICE 3

Work in groups. Tell the group something interesting about your partner.

Example: Jodi always washes her car on Saturday morning.

2. Talking about routines (2)

Do you ever	play sports on the weekend? go out on Saturday night?	Yes, I	sometimes play tennis. often go out on Saturday night.
		I do sometimes. / I sometimes do.	
		No,	not very often. I never do.
Does she ever	play sports on the weekend? go out on Saturday night?	Yes, she	sometimes plays tennis / sports. often goes out.
		She does sometimes.	
		No,	not very often. she never does.

PRACTICE 1

Class CD 2
Track 5

Listen to the example. Do you do these things on Saturday night? How often? Ask and answer questions with a partner.

1. go out with friends
2. go out with your parents
3. watch a midnight movie
4. go out to eat

5. go to a movie on your own
6. go dancing
7. have friends over for a party
8. stay home and watch TV

PRACTICE 2

What are some other things you do on Saturday night? Write three things below, then ask your partner. Reverse roles.

1. I sometimes _____
2. I often _____
3. I usually _____

A: I sometimes play video games all night.
    Do you ever do that?
B: No way!

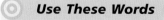

Use These Words

read a book
play video games
study for school
go shopping
listen to music
clean the house

LISTEN TO THIS

Class CD 2
Track 6

Part 1 Listen to Angie and Ivan talking about Angie's work. How does she like her job? Check (✓) the best phrase.

___ hates it   ___ it's OK   ___ likes it a lot

Part 2 Listen again. Check (✓) if these statements are True or False.

		True	False
1	gets up at 5 A.M.		
2	a car takes her to the location		
3	often spends eight hours on a photo shoot		
4	sometimes gets home very late		
5	always gets to keep the clothes she models		
6	sometimes makes $1,000 for a day's work		

Part 3 Would you like to be a model? Talk with a partner about the pros and cons (good points and bad points) of modeling.

LET'S TALK

Part 1 What do you do at these times? Complete the chart with information about yourself.

	What do you do...?	Me	Classmate
1	on a long weekend		
2	on a hot summer's day		
3	on a cold winter's day		
4	on a public holiday		
5	on your birthday		

Part 2 Interview your classmates to find out what they do at these times. When you find someone who does the same things as you do, write his or her name in the chart.

A: What do you do on a public holiday?
B: I usually sleep in late. Then I sometimes…

Use These Words

I sleep late, too.
So do I.
I do, too.
I don't either.
Neither do I.

Conversation 2

How was your weekend?

What's your favorite place to go on the weekend?

Class CD 2, Track 7

Jack: How was your weekend, Mei-ho?
Mei-ho: It was pretty good, thanks. How about you? Did you have a nice weekend?
Jack: Yes, it was terrific.
Mei-ho: What did you do?
Jack: I went to the beach with my family. It was great.
Mei-ho: How was the weather?
Jack: Fantastic—sunny and hot.
Mei-ho: So what did you do there?
Jack: We walked along the beach and swam in the ocean. And then we had a barbecue on the beach on Saturday night. On Sunday I played tennis.
Mei-ho: Oh…so that's why you're so sunburned!

Student CD, Track 15

Class CD 2, Track 8
Pronunciation Focus

Listen to how *was* is pronounced in these sentences.

How was your weekend?
It was pretty good.
How was the weather?
It was terrific.

Listen to the conversation again and notice the pronunciation of *was*.

GIVE IT A TRY

1. Asking about the weekend

How was your weekend?	It was	great. terrific. OK. pretty good. very quiet.	How was yours?

PRACTICE

**Class CD 2
Track 9** — Listen to the example. Work in groups. Greet your classmates and ask about the weekend. Switch roles.

2. Talking about past events (1)

		Regular verbs	Irregular verbs
What did you do	on the weekend? last night?	I watched a DVD. I visited friends. I stayed in.	I went to the beach. I swam in the ocean.

PRACTICE

**Class CD 2
Track 10** — Listen to the example. Check (✓) if you did any of these things last weekend. Then ask your partner what he or she did. Reverse roles.

___ saw a movie
___ went shopping
___ surfed the web
___ went to a party
___ played basketball
___ relaxed
___ studied
___ met friends
___ your idea _____

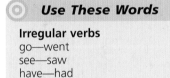

Use These Words

Irregular verbs
go—went
see—saw
have—had
buy—bought

3. Talking about past events (2)

Did you have a nice weekend?	Yes, I did.
Did you go to the movies on Sunday?	No, I didn't. I went shopping.

PRACTICE

Class CD 2 Track 11 Listen to the example. Did you do any of these things last weekend? Write *yes* or *no*, and add details in the chart. Then ask a partner questions about his or her weekend. Reverse roles.

Did you...?	Me	My partner
go shopping		
send any e-mails		
play sports		
sleep late		
go out with friends		
clean your room		
watch a movie		

LISTEN TO THIS

Class CD 2 Track 12 *Part 1* Listen to the conversation. What are Sami and Tamika talking about? Check (✔) the best answer.

___ movies   ___ music   ___ weekends   ___ sports

Part 2 Listen again. What did Sami and Tamika do on the weekend? Check (✔) the things they did.

		Sami	Tamika
1	Went to a concert		
2	Saw a movie		
3	Went to a party		
4	Studied for a test		
5	Played soccer		
6	What else?		

Part 3 Listen again. What else did they do? Write your answers above.

Part 4 Talk about Sami's and Tamika's weekends with a partner. How was your weekend similar or different?

PERSON TO PERSON STUDENTS A AND B

Part 1 Complete the chart below with information about yourself.

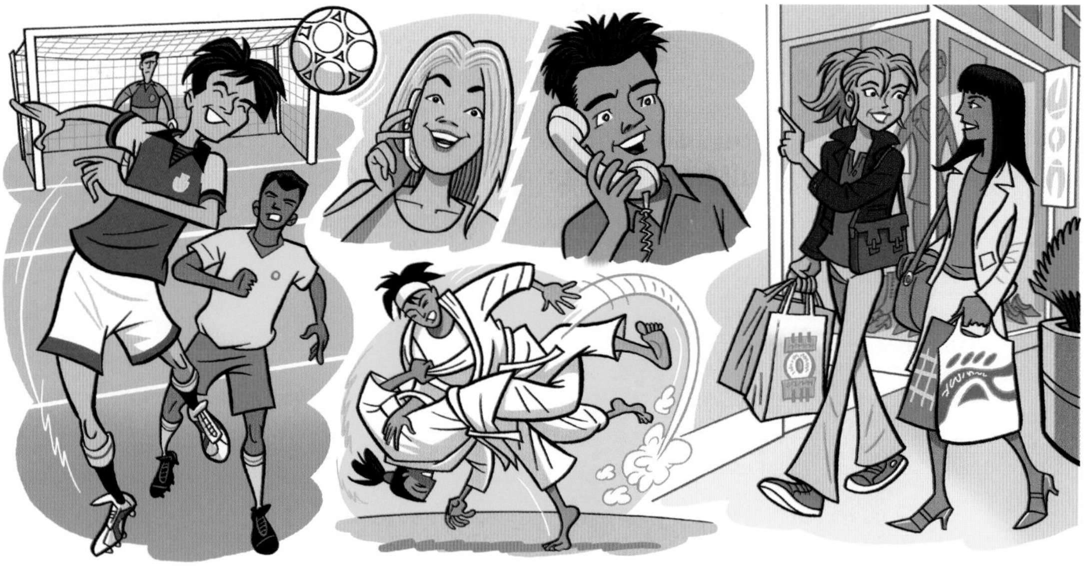

What is something...?	Me	My partner
1 you usually do on Saturday morning		
2 you never do on Sunday		
3 you often do after class		
4 you often talk about with your best friend		
5 you bought last week		
6 different you did last week		
7 you did last weekend but you didn't enjoy		

Part 2 Interview your partner and take notes in the chart. Then compare your answers.

Now Try This

What are some things that often happen in your city or town on the weekend? What are things visitors often like to do and see? Talk about them with a partner.

Unit 8

Conversation 1
Do you like coffee?

What do you usually have for breakfast? Do you have a small breakfast or a big breakfast?

CONSIDER THIS

Breakfast foods around the world

Bolivia *salteña* is a pastry filled with meat, vegetables, olives, and raisins

Madagascar *kitoza* is dried beef cooked over a fire

Singapore *nasi lemak* is a dish made with rice, coconut milk, and fish

● Which foods would you like to try?

Class CD 2, Track 13

Mike: What do you usually have for breakfast at home, Kenny?
Kenny: I usually have rice and soup.
Mike: Yeah? And what do you have to drink?
Kenny: Oh, I usually have juice or milk.
Mike: Do you like coffee?
Kenny: Yes, it's OK. But I don't drink a lot of coffee.
Mike: What's your favorite drink?
Kenny: I guess it's soda.

Student CD, Track 16

1. Asking about meals

What do you have for breakfast?	I usually have	toast and fruit.
		rice and eggs.
		bread and fruit.
	I don't usually eat breakfast.	
Where do you have lunch?	I have lunch	at school.
		at home.
		in the cafeteria.

PRACTICE 1

Look at things people sometimes have for breakfast or lunch. With a partner, think of some other foods and add them to the chart.

Breakfast	Lunch	Drinks
rice	noodles	tea
eggs	sandwiches	coffee
fruit	fast food	juice
bread	sushi	water
toast	a burger	milk
soup	a salad	soda

PRACTICE 2

Class CD 2
Track 14

Listen to the example. Talk with a partner about what you have for breakfast and lunch.

A: What do you have for breakfast?
B: I usually have _____. What about you?
A: I usually have _____. And what do you have to drink?
B: _____. And what do you have for lunch?
A: Oh, I usually have _____. What do you have?
B: I have _____ or maybe _____.
A: Where do you have lunch?
B: I usually have lunch _____.

2. Asking about likes

Do you like coffee?	Yes, it's OK. / Yes, I do.
	Yes, but I don't drink a lot of coffee.
	No, I don't. / Not really.
What's your favorite	drink?	I guess it's soda.
	food?	I really like pizza.

PRACTICE 1

Class CD 2 Track 15

Listen to the example. Look at the foods and drinks below. Do you like them? Ask your partner about them. Reverse roles.

coffee

soda

soy milk

yogurt

cheese

spicy food

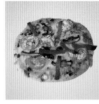
pizza

lamb

seafood

brownies

A: Do you like coffee?
B: Not really. What about you?
A: Yes, I do.

PRACTICE 2

Complete the chart with information about yourself. Then ask a partner about their favorites. Reverse roles.

	What's your favorite...?	
1	type of food (for example, Italian or Thai)	
2	dessert	
3	sandwich	
4	fast food	
5	snack	

Use These Words

Thai	cake
Mexican	cookies
Korean	brownies
Japanese	pie
Indian	ice cream
French	
Chinese	
Vietnamese	

LISTEN TO THIS

Class CD 2
Track 16

Part 1 Aran and Robert are comparing what they eat in Thailand and in England. Which meal are they talking about?

___ breakfast   ___ lunch   ___ dinner   ___ snacks

Part 2 Listen again. What do people in Thailand and England usually have for breakfast? Check (✔) the things they say.

	Thailand	England		Thailand	England
Bacon			Juice		
Beef curry			Mushrooms		
Boiled eggs			Rice		
Cereal			Sausages		
Chicken curry			Tomatoes		
Coffee			Toast		
Fried eggs			Tea		
Fruit			Vegetables		

Part 3 Listen again. What do Aran and Robert usually have for breakfast? Mark the items with an ✗.

Part 4 Do you eat any of the same foods? Talk with your partner about what you have for breakfast.

LET'S TALK

Part 1 You are going to do a survey. First fill in the chart with information about yourself.

	Me	Classmate
Favorite meat		
Favorite fish		
Favorite fruit		
Favorite fast food		
Favorite holiday food		
Favorite meal		
Your idea:		

Part 2 Work in groups. Ask your classmates about their favorites.

A: What's your favorite meat?
B: I guess it's chicken. What's yours?
A: Lamb.
B: Really? I don't like lamb very much.

Part 3 Do you and your classmates like the same foods?

Conversation 2
Are you hungry?

Are there any cafes or restaurants near your school? What kind of food do they serve?

Class CD 2, Track 17

Jodi:	Are you hungry?
Kenny:	Yes, I am.
Jodi:	Me too. Let's have something to eat.
Kenny:	What do you feel like?
Jodi:	How about some cake and a cappuccino?
Kenny:	OK.
Jodi:	Let's go to the Starlight Cafe. They have delicious cakes and great cappuccino.
Kenny:	That sounds good. Let's go.

Student CD, Track 17

Class CD 2, Track 18
Pronunciation Focus

Notice the intonation of these questions.

Are you hungry?

What do you feel like?

How about some cake and a cappuccino?

Listen to the conversation again and notice the intonation of the quest

GIVE IT A TRY

1. Asking about wants and preferences

Informally		
Are you	hungry?	Yes, I am.
	thirsty?	Not right now.
What do you feel like?		Maybe a milk shake.
How about a coffee?		No, thanks.
More formally		
Would you like something to eat / drink?		Yes, please. / No, thank you.
What would you like to eat?		I'd like a burger.
What would she like to drink?		She would like some juice.
Would you like some water?		Yes, please.

PRACTICE 1

Class CD 2
Track 19

Listen to the example. Ask a partner what he or she feels like having.
Reverse roles.

an ice-cream sundae   **a milk shake**   **some noodles**

some sushi   **some soup**   **iced tea**

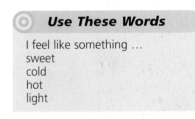

Use These Words

I feel like something …
sweet
cold
hot
light

PRACTICE 2

Class CD 2
Track 20

Listen to the example. Now ask your partner more formally. Reverse roles.

A: Would you like something to eat?
B: No, not right now.
A: Would you like something to drink?
B: Yes, please. I'd like a milk shake.

Work in groups. You are going out to buy lunch, dinner, or a snack for three classmates. Ask what they want to eat and drink and write their answers below. Reverse roles.

Name	Food	Drink

Now compare your answers with someone from another group.

Example: Ali would like pizza and a soda.
Silvia would like sushi and iced tea.

LISTEN TO THIS

Class CD 2
Track 21

Part 1 Listen to people placing orders in a cafe. What meal are they eating?

___ breakfast   ___ lunch   ___ dinner

Part 2 Listen again and mark their orders. Write *M* next to the things Maria orders, and *P* next to the things Paul orders.

Menu

Fresh Salads
___ Mixed green salad $5.95   ___ Pasta salad $6.95
___ Chicken salad $7.50   ___ Seafood salad $8.50

All salads served with bread and choice of dressings: Italian, Sesame, Ranch

Sandwiches
___ Club sandwich $7.25   ___ Grilled vegetable $5.75
___ Tuna sandwich $5.95   ___ Toasted cheese sandwich $4.50

Side Dishes   **Desserts**
___ French fries $2.95   ___ Chocolate cake $3.50
___ Fruit salad $3.50   ___ Apple pie $3.50
___ Three bean salad $3.75

Beverages
___ Iced coffee $2.00   ___ Coffee $1.50
___ Iced tea $2.00   ___ Tea $1.50
          ___ Juice (apple, grapefruit, orange, tomato) $1.50

Part 3 Work in groups of three. Role-play the conversation between Maria and Paul and the server.

(Student A looks at this page. Student B looks at page 110.)

Part 1 You are traveling in Australia. You stop for breakfast at a cafe. Ask what they have to eat and drink. Fill in the menu.

Breakfast Menu

Eggs
Prepared to order:

_____, _____, _____, *or* _____

Waffles
Homemade waffles served with fresh
_____ (_____, _____, *or* _____)

Beverages
Tea, Coffee
Juice *Choice of* _____, _____, *or* _____

Milk

Omelettes
Made with _____ *eggs.*
Choice of fillings: _____, _____, *or* _____

From the Bakery
Muffins *Choice of* _____, _____, *or* _____

Croissant *Served with* _____ *or* _____

Part 2 Decide what you want for breakfast—choose something to eat and something to drink. Tell your partner.

Part 3 Reverse roles. You are the server, and your partner is the customer. Take your partner's order. Take notes.

Now Try This

Work with your partner. Prepare a simple breakfast menu for a cafe in your country. Then use your menu and role-play ordering breakfast.

Conversation 1
You are really creative.

What hobbies do you enjoy? Do you collect anything?

CONSIDER THIS

Creative careers

At New Zealand's National Institute of Creative Arts and Industries you can study:

Painting   Photography
Dance   Music

- Would you like to study any of these?
- Do you do any of these as hobbies?

Class CD 2, Track 22

Aya: Congratulations, Julia. You are a really good photographer.

Julia: Thanks.

Aya: So how do you take a good photograph?

Julia: Well, you need to be patient. It takes time to get a good picture. You need good light and a good subject.

Aya: And I guess you need to be creative. Your photos are always very original.

Julia: Well, I try to be different.

Aya: I never seem to take good photos. I don't think I'm very artistic. And I'm not very patient.

Julia: Well, it's easy to learn. Do you want me to give you some lessons?

Aya: Yeah. That would be great.

Student CD, Track 18

GIVE IT A TRY

1. Describing qualities

| A photographer needs to be patient. | He / She also needs to be | artistic.
creative.
original. |

PRACTICE 1

Class CD 2
Track 23

Listen to the example. What qualities do these people need? Choose three for each person. Then talk about your answers with a partner.

A: I think a teacher needs to be well-organized, energetic, and smart.
B: I think a teacher needs to be well-organized, flexible, and tolerant.

a teacher

a parent

a best friend

an employer

Use These Words

easygoing	understanding
creative	flexible
smart	funny
energetic	serious
generous	well-organized
reliable	tolerant

PRACTICE 2

Class CD 2
Track 24

Listen to the example. What positive and negative qualities do you have? Complete the chart for yourself. Then talk about your answers with a partner.

My positive qualities	My negative qualities

Example: I'm patient and easygoing. But sometimes I'm forgetful.

Use These Words

smart	funny
lazy	forgetful
sloppy	patient
neat	emotional

2. Asking about abilities and talents

Are you creative?		I think so. Somewhat. No, I'm not (very creative).
Are you good at	languages? math?	Yes, I am. I'm pretty good at languages / math. Not really.

PRACTICE 1

Check (✓) your skills in the chart below.

What are your special talents?

A Are you: ☐ **Creative** ☐ **Artistic** ☐ **Musical**

B Are you good at:

☐ **Singing** ☐ **Sports** ☐ **Math** ☐ **Dancing** ☐ **Languages**

☐ **Poetry** ☐ **Drama** ☐ **Debates** ☐ **Painting** ☐ **Story-telling**

PRACTICE 2

Class CD 2 Track 25

Listen to the example. Work in pairs. Ask your partner questions about the talents and skills in Practice 1. Reverse roles.

PRACTICE 3

Work in groups. Talk about your partner's special talents or abilities.

Example: Yoshi is very artistic. He's also good at singing.

LISTEN TO THIS

Part 1 Carl is talking about his family. Listen and check (✓) the people he is talking about.

___ brother   ___ father   ___ sister   ___ mother

Part 2 Check (✓) the correct information about each person's talents and skills.

	Sports	Languages	Math	Music	Computers	Dancing
Rosa						
Peter						

Part 3 Talk to your partner about Rosa and Peter (Carl's brother). Describe them. Who are you most similar to?

LET'S TALK

Part 1 Complete the chart with information about the people below.

		My mother	My father	My best friend
1	What special talents do they have?			
2	What are some of their positive qualities?			
3	Do they have any negative qualities?			
4	What are some things they are good at?			
5	What are some things they are not good at?			

Part 2 Ask your partner questions about the people above. Reverse roles.

Conversation 2
Can you play the guitar?

What musical instruments are popular in your country? Do you play an instrument?

Class CD 2, Track 27

Tim: Wow! You can play the guitar really well.
Aya: Thanks. Can you play the guitar?
Tim: No, I can't. But I can play the violin.
Aya: Really? What else can you play?
Tim: I can play the trumpet, too.
Aya: Oh, yeah? I can't play the trumpet. I think it's pretty hard.
Tim: It's not that hard. You just need to practice.
Aya: Can I hear you play some time?
Tim: Sure.

Student CD, Track 19

Class CD 2, Track 28
Pronunciation Focus

Notice how *can* and *can't* are pronounced.

Can you play the guitar?
I can play the guitar.
I can't play the trumpet.

Listen to the conversation again and notice the pronunciation of *can* and *can't*.

1. Describing abilities (1)

Can you play the guitar?	Yes, I can. No, I can't.
Can Tim play the piano?	Yes, he can. No, he can't.

I Rosa	can play the	piano, but I violin, but she	can't play the	trumpet. guitar.

I can't play the piano very well.

PRACTICE 1

Class CD 2
Track 29

Work in groups. Listen to the example. How many of these things can you do? Check (✓) your answers. Then ask and answer questions with your partners.

		Yes	Not very well	No
1	Play hockey			
2	Play chess			
3	Play tennis			
4	Sing			
5	Dance			
6	Cook			
7	Play the piano			
8	Play the guitar			
9	Play the violin			

A: Can you play hockey?
B: No, I can't. Can you?
A: Not very well.

PRACTICE 2

Tell the class two things people in your group can do and two things they can't do.

2. Describing abilities (2)

What	musical instrument	can you play?	I can play the guitar.
	else		
What languages can you speak?			I can speak Chinese.

PRACTICE 1

Class CD 2
Track 30

Work in groups. Listen to the example. Talk to three classmates and complete the chart with information about them.

	Name:	1 _____	2 _____	3 _____
1	What languages can you speak?			
2	What sports can you play?			
3	What instruments can you play?			
4	What dishes can you cook?			
5	What dances can you do?			

PRACTICE 2

Tell the class three facts about your classmates.

Example: Daniel can dance the tango. Sun-woo can play the electric guitar.

LISTEN TO THIS

Class CD 2
Track 31

Part 1 Listen to Sonia and Mike. Where are they? Check (✔) the correct answer.

___ home   ___ cafe   ___ school   ___ library   ___ concert

Part 2 Listen again. Circle their answers to questions about languages, music, and sports.

		Sonia	Mike
1	What languages can they speak?	French Chinese Spanish	German Japanese Korean
2	What instruments can they play?	piano violin guitar	organ guitar drums
3	What sports can they play?	tennis soccer basketball	judo tennis baseball

Part 3 How well can they do the things above? Write ✚ for things they do well and − for things they're not good at. With a partner, compare your abilities with Sonia's and Mike's.

(Student A looks at this page. Student B looks at page 111.)

Part 1 Look at these two ads for summer jobs. What special skills or abilities do you think a person would need for each job? Choose from the box and add your own ideas. Write *R* next to the skills a reporter needs. Write *B* next to the skills a baby-sitter needs.

Summer Jobs Available

Reporter for college magazine   Baby-sitter on cruise ship

good at languages ____	flexible ____
good at English ____	persuasive ____
a good communicator ____	good IT skills ____
good at sports ____	good sense of humor ____
creative ____	sings well ____
patient ____	plays a musical instrument ____
your idea _____	your idea _____

Part 2 Your partner is interested in applying for one of the jobs above. Ask about his or her skills. Tell your partner which job you think is best for him or her.

Part 3 You are interested in applying for one of the jobs below. Decide which one you think you are most qualified for.

Summer Jobs Available

Sales assistant in music store   Telephone-marketing salesperson for health foods

Part 4 Your partner will ask you about your skills. Answer the questions and find out which job is best for you.

Now Try This

What hobbies and pastimes do people enjoy that are special to your country? Do they require any special skills or abilities?

Review:
Units 7–9

LISTEN TO THIS   UNIT 7

Class CD 2
Track 32

Part 1 Ken is talking about his vacation. How were these things? Listen and check (✓) his responses.

		Good	So-so	Not good
1	The hotel			
2	The weather			
3	The flight			

Part 2 Ask your partner questions to find out if your answers are the same.

GIVE IT A TRY

Work with a partner. Ask and answer these questions. Ask follow-up questions of your own.

1. How do you usually spend your free time?
2. What do you often do when you go out with friends?
3. What is something you never do on the weekend?
4. What is something you sometimes do in the evening?
5. What is something you always do in the morning?

LISTEN TO THIS   UNIT 8

Class CD 2
Track 33

Part 1 Jay and Sally are trying to decide where to eat. Check (✓) what kind of food the places below serve. What is their food like?

		The menu						Their food	
		Cake	Sandwiches	Pizza	Noodles	Hot dogs	Sushi	Great	So-so
1	Jenny's Kitchen								
2	Bob's Cafe								
3	The Snack Shack								

Part 2 Where do they decide to eat? Ask your partner questions to find out if your answers are the same.

Work with a group. Ask the people in your group about their favorite food and drink. Write their answers below. Do people in your group like the same things?

1. Favorite foods: _____

2. Favorite drinks: _____

LISTEN TO THIS   UNIT 9

Class CD 2
Track 34

Part 1 Cassy is trying to find a roommate. She's telling a friend about two people she has met. Listen and check (✔) each person's qualities.

		Cassy	Kavita	Soon-Ya
1	Well-organized			
2	Lazy			
3	Sloppy			
4	Serious			
5	Funny			
6	Easygoing			
7	Energetic			
8	Reliable			
9	Flexible			
10	Creative			
11	Forgetful			

Part 2 Who do you think Cassy should choose?

GIVE IT A TRY

Work with a partner. Ask each other the questions below. Then suggest a good job for each other.

1. Are you persuasive? Can you sell people things?
2. Are you a good communicator? Can you give speeches in public?
3. Are you a problem solver? Can you help people with problems?
4. Are you creative? Can you make things?
5. Are you artistic? Can you draw or paint?
6. Are you organized? Can you work on different things at the same time?
7. Are you easygoing? Can you work well under stress?

Unit 10

Conversation 1
Let's have coffee.

Do you like to visit coffee shops? What do you like to drink?

It's the world's most popular drink. Every day, people drink about 2,000,000,000 cups! Men drink about 1.7 cups a day. Women drink about 1.5 cups.
The US drinks more coffee than any other country—over 1,000,000 kg of coffee beans each year.

- Do you like coffee?
- What's your favorite drink?

Class CD 2, Track 35

Arun: I'd love some coffee. Is there a coffee shop around here?

Beth: Yeah, there's one just around the corner.

Arun: Really? Whereabouts?

Beth: It's next to the bookstore. It's called Dove.

Arun: Oh, yeah. Do you feel like having a cup of coffee?

Beth: Sure. And after that I'd like to have a look at that new music store.

Arun: Where's that?

Beth: It's on Forbes Street, near the subway entrance.

Arun: OK. Sounds good.

Student CD, Track 20

1. Asking about places

Is there a	coffee shop around music store near	here?	No, I don't think so. Yes, there is. On Pine Street. Yes, there's one on Pine Street, next to… There's a coffee shop on Pine Street.

PRACTICE 1

Class CD 2
Track 36

Listen to the example. Ask your partner about the places below. Reverse roles.

1. a supermarket
2. a drugstore
3. a newsstand

4. a movie theater
5. a subway entrance
6. a bookstore

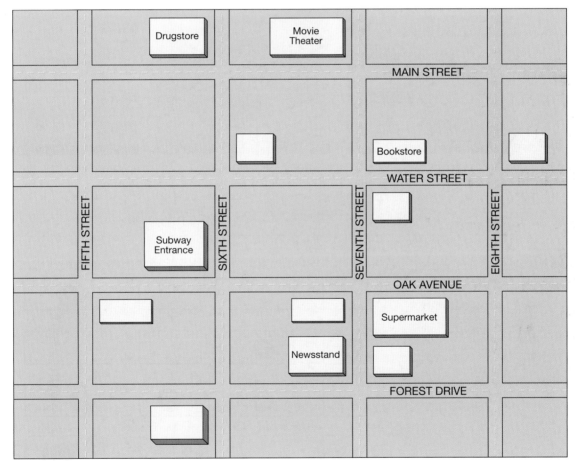

PRACTICE 2

Ask your partner about places in your neighborhood.
Reverse roles.

A: Is there a bus stop near here?
B: Yes, there's one on Main Street.

Use These Words

bus stop
restaurant
bank
shopping mall
coffee shop
ATM (automated teller machine)

2. Describing outdoor locations

Where's	the coffee shop?
	that?
Whereabouts?	

It's **on** Pine Street.

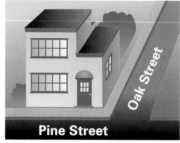

It's **on the corner of** Pine and Oak.

It's **next to** the bookstore.

It's **across from** the supermarket.

It's **near** the train station.

It's **between** the bank and the hotel.

PRACTICE 1

Class CD 2 Track 37

Listen to the example. Take turns asking about the location of the places below.

1. coffee shop
2. movie theater
3. drugstore
4. post office
5. bank
6. department store
7. music store

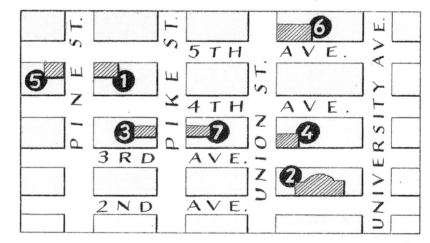

PRACTICE 2

Ask and answer questions like these:

A: What's on Pine Street, across from the bank?

B: The...

LISTEN TO THIS

Class CD 2
Track 38

Part 1 Listen to two people talking. What does the first person want to know?

Part 2 Listen again and mark the location of these places on the map.

1. bookstore   3. hairdresser   5. Chinese restaurant

2. Indian restaurant   4. gym   6. coffee shop

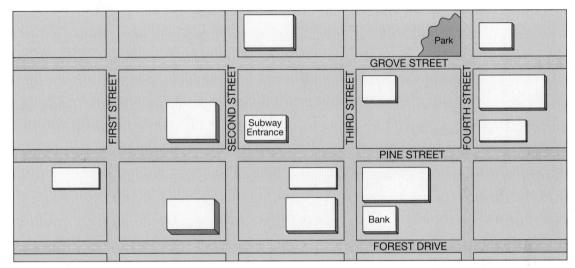

Part 3 Does the man recommend each place or not? Talk about it with your partner and write a (✓) next to the places he likes.

LET'S TALK

Part 1 Work with a partner. Draw a map of your school neighborhood showing a few of the main streets. Mark the location of five places you know on the map.

Example: There's a photo shop here, on the corner.

Part 2 Compare your map with others. How many different places can you identify?

Conversation 2
How do I get there?

How do you get around your city? Which forms of transportation do you use?

Class CD 2, Track 39

Arun: You check the map and I'll drive.

Kim: OK. Go down this street for about three blocks. You are going to turn at the next intersection.

Arun: Do I turn right or left?

Kim: Sorry. Turn left after the drugstore.

Arun: OK. Now what?

Kim: Now we go along this street for three blocks. Their building is number 366.

Arun: There it is. But where can we park the car?

Kim: There's a parking lot just down the street, across from the supermarket.

Student CD, Track 21

Class CD 2, Track 40
Pronunciation Focus

Notice how we pronounce compound nouns—the first word gets more stress.

drugstore
parking lot
supermarket

Listen to the conversation again and notice the stress in the compound nouns.

GIVE IT A TRY

1. Giving directions

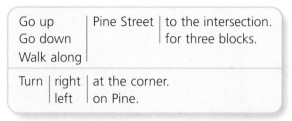

Go up	Pine Street	to the intersection.
Go down		for three blocks.
Walk along		

| Turn | right | at the corner. |
| | left | on Pine. |

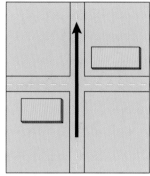
Go up / down the street.

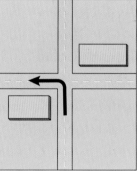
Turn left.

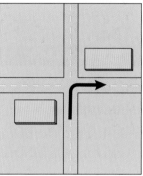
Turn right.

PRACTICE 1

Class CD 2
Track 41

Listen to the example. Give your partner directions. Your partner names the picture you are describing. Reverse roles.

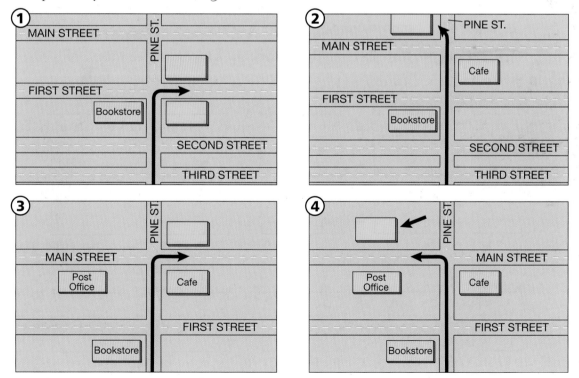

Class CD 2
Track 42

Listen to the example. You are at **X**. Ask your partner how to get to the places below. Reverse roles.

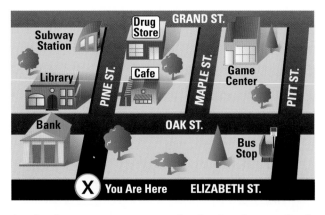

1. the bus stop   3. the bank   5. the game center   7. the library
2. the subway station   4. the cafe   6. the drugstore

A: How do I get to the bus stop? / I'm looking for…
B: OK. Go along Pine Street…

LISTEN TO THIS

Class CD 2
Track 43

Part 1 Listen to someone ask for directions. Which place does the person *not* ask directions to?

___ cafe   ___ drugstore   ___ shoe store
___ club   ___ train station   ___ music store

Part 2 Listen to the directions and mark the places on the map with an **X** and label them.

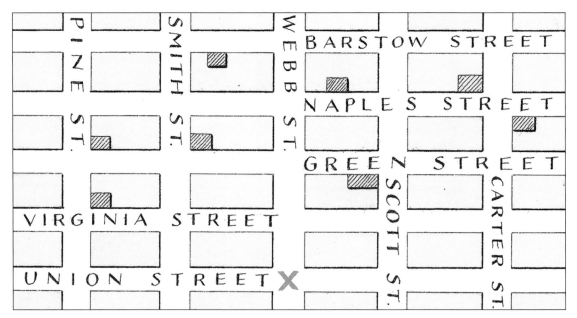

Part 3 Tell your partner where you are standing and ask for directions from there to one of the places on the map.

(Student A looks at this page. Student B looks at page 112.)

Part 1 Look at your map. You are new in town. Ask your partner about these places: cafe, bookstore, post office, bank. Label them on your map. You are both at ✗.

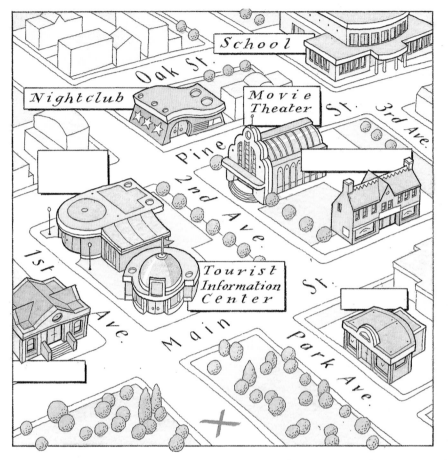

Part 2 Answer your partner's questions about these places: a nightclub, a school, a tourist information center, a movie theater.

Part 3 Ask your partner how to get to these places: a hairdresser, a travel agency, a museum.

Conversation 1
Could you lend me $20?

Do friends sometimes borrow things from you?
What kind of things?

CONSIDER THIS

Proverbs about borrowing

"Borrowed clothes never fit w
"When you borrow, you are n
free."
"Lenders have better memorie
than borrowers."

- Do you borrow things?
- What do you borrow?
- What do people borrow
  from you?

Class CD 2, Track 44

Ben:	Hi, Wade. How are things?
Wade:	Pretty good, thanks. How are you?
Ben:	I'm fine. By the way, can I borrow your digital camera tonight? I have to take some photos for my class project.
Wade:	Sure. No problem.
Ben:	Thanks a lot.
Wade:	You're welcome.
Ben:	Oh, one more thing. Could you lend me $20 until the weekend? I'm broke.
Wade:	Sorry, I can't. I'm broke, too!

Student CD, Track 22

GIVE IT A TRY

1. Asking to borrow things

Informally		
Can I borrow your	camera? pen?	Sure. No problem. All right.
Can you lend me your	camera? pen?	OK.
More formally		
Could you lend me $20?		Yes, of course.
Would you be able to lend me $20?		
Could I borrow your pen?		
Do you think I could borrow your book?		

PRACTICE 1

Class CD 2
Track 45

Listen to the example. Take turns requesting the things below. Your partner accepts the requests.

A: Can I borrow your…?

B: Can you lend me your…?

digital camera

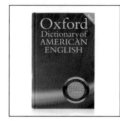

dictionary

laptop

cell phone

bicycle

DVD player

calculator

binoculars

PRACTICE 2

Class CD 2
Track 46

Think of three more things you want to borrow from classmates and write them below. Listen to the example. Then ask classmates if you can borrow them or if they will lend them to you. This time ask more formally.

1. _____   2. _____   3. _____

2. Declining requests and giving a reason

Can I borrow your pen?	Sorry, but I'm using it.
Can you lend me $10?	Oh, sorry. I can't. I'm broke!
Do you think I could borrow your laptop?	Sorry, I'm using it (right now).

PRACTICE 1

Class CD 2
Track 47

Listen to the example. Practice making the requests below. Your partner declines and gives a reason. Reverse roles.

Use These Words

didn't bring it today
need it myself
using it
have a lot of bills to pay
it's not working

1. borrow your car for the weekend
2. lend me $100 until the end of the month
3. let me use your laptop tonight
4. borrow your cell phone
5. use your calculator

PRACTICE 2

Class CD 2
Track 48

Listen to the example. Think of three more requests and write them below. Then practice making your requests. Your classmates decline and give reasons. Reverse roles.

1. _____
2. _____
3. _____

LISTEN TO THIS

Class CD 2
Track 49

Part 1 Listen to people making requests. What do they want to borrow? Number the items in the chart from 1–6.

		Accept	Refuse			Accept	Refuse
___	laptop			___	bicycle		
___	camera			___	tennis racket		
___	book			___	CD player		

Part 2 Listen again. Does each person accept the request or refuse it? Check (✓) the correct column.

Part 3 Talk with a partner. Would you feel comfortable asking a classmate for these things? How about a family member?

LET'S TALK

Part 1 Read the questions below and answer them with a partner.

> 1. What kinds of things do you sometimes borrow from these people?
>   a) your parents   b) your brothers or sisters   c) your friends
>
> 2. Would you ever lend these things to friends?
>   a) money   b) your laptop   c) clothes   d) books or magazines
>
> 3. Have you borrowed anything from your friends recently?
>
> 4. What are some things you would never lend a friend?

Part 2 Your partner will ask to borrow these things. Think of a reason to say no to each request. Reverse roles.

1. your bicycle
2. your new jacket
3. your DVD player

Conversation 2
Let's have a party!

How do you celebrate your birthday?
Do you get presents?

Class CD 2, Track 50

Patty: When is your birthday, Wade?
Wade: Actually it's next week. On Thursday.
Patty: Really? What are your plans?
Wade: Well, do you mind if I invite a few friends over for a small party?
Patty: That's fine. How many friends do you want to invite?
Wade: Maybe five or six.
Patty: Sure. That's no problem.
Wade: And is it all right if we use the kitchen and cook a meal?
Patty: Of course. You can cook dinner any time you like!

Student CD, Track 23

Class CD 2, Track 51
Pronunciation Focus

Wh- questions often have falling intonation. Listen to the intonation in these questions.

When is your birthday?
What are your plans?

Listen to the conversation again and notice the intonation of the questions.

1. Asking for and giving permission

Informally		
Can I Is it OK if I	invite my friends over next week?	Yes, that's fine. Sure. No problem.
More formally		
Do you mind Is it all right	if I have a party on Sunday?	Sure. That's OK. Of course.

PRACTICE 1

Class CD 2
Track 52

Listen to the example. You are staying at a friend's house. You want permission to do the following things. Add your own idea. Then ask your partner for permission informally. Reverse roles.

1. make a cup of coffee
2. use the phone
3. watch the TV
4. have a look at the newspaper
5. take a shower
6. (your idea) _____

PRACTICE 2

Now ask a different partner about the things in Practice 1. This time ask more formally. Reverse roles.

2. Declining permission and giving a reason

Do you mind if I watch TV?	Sorry, I'm trying to read.
Is it all right if I use the phone?	Sorry. I'm waiting for a call. Well, maybe later if you don't mind.

PRACTICE 1

Class CD 2
Track 53

Listen to the example. You are a houseguest, and your partner is your host. Ask your partner to do the things below. Your partner declines and gives a reason. Reverse roles.

1. change the TV channel
2. do my laundry
3. have a look at today's paper
4. cook myself something to eat
5. take a nap in the living room

Use These Words

do it later
still reading it
waiting to see the news
need to use the kitchen for a while
better to lie down in the bedroom

PRACTICE 2

Think of three more requests a houseguest might make. Practice asking and declining them with a partner. Reverse roles.

LISTEN TO THIS

Class CD 2
Track 54

Part 1 Listen to someone asking permission to do things. Where are they?

___ at a friend's house   ___ at school   ___ at a hotel

Part 2 Listen again. Does the other person agree to the request or not? Check (✔) the illustrations of the requests he or she agrees to.

(Student A looks at this page. Student B looks at page 113.)

Part 1 You want to borrow the things below from your roommate. Check (✓) the one he or she agrees to lend you, and write down the excuses he or she offers for the others.

		Agrees	Doesn't agree	Excuse
1	surfboard			
2	goggles			
3	motorcycle			

Part 2 Your roommate asks for permission to do three things. Agree to one but not the others. Give a reason for saying no.

Part 3 Change partners. This time you are student B.

Now Try This

Someone wants to borrow money, your tennis racket, and your magazine. Think of excuses for not lending these items.

Conversation 1

How was your year?

Did you enjoy this year? What are some of the things you did?

Class CD 2, Track 55

Yi-lin: So did you have a good year, Andy?

Andy: Yeah, it was pretty good, thanks. How about you?

Yi-lin: I had a good year, too.

Andy: Did you do anything special this year?

Yi-lin: Well, I took a judo class. That was fun. And you?

Andy: I went to Canada for a vacation. It was terrific.

Yi-lin: What was your best experience in Canada?

Andy: On the ski slopes. I went skiing every day. I really enjoyed it.

Yi-lin: That's great. And I hope next year is even better.

1. Talking about past experiences (1)

Did you have a good year?	Yes, I did. It was ⎰pretty good, thanks. ⎱OK.
Did you ⎰do anything⎱ interesting? ⎰go anywhere⎱	Yes, ⎰I took a judo class. ⎱I went to Canada.
	No, not really.

PRACTICE 1

Class CD 2 Track 56

Listen to the example. Check (✔) the things you did this year. Then talk with a partner. Use follow-up questions to ask for more information. Reverse roles.

Did you...?		Follow-up questions
1 **Go anywhere interesting**	☐	Where did you go?
2 **Take any classes**	☐	What class did you take?
3 **Read any good books**	☐	What did you read?
4 **See any good movies**	☐	What movies did you see?
5 **Buy anything special**	☐	What was it?
6 **Try any new foods**	☐	How was it?
7 **Make any new friends**	☐	Where did you meet?

PRACTICE 2

Work with a different partner. Tell him or her something interesting you learned about your partner in Practice 1.

Example: Kerry went to Canada for vacation. He went skiing every day.

2. Talking about past experiences (2)

Did you do anything special?	Yes. I got a new job.
	No, not really.
What was your	best	experience?	My trip to the US. I went to San Francisco for a week.
	worst		I had an accident on my bike and broke my arm.

PRACTICE

Class CD 2
Track 57 Fill in the chart with information about yourself. Listen to the example.
Then ask and answer questions with a partner.

1	Did you do anything special?	
2	Did you do anything exciting?	
3	Did you do anything dangerous?	
4	What was your best experience?	
5	What was your worst experience?	

LISTEN TO THIS

Class CD 2
Track 58

Part 1 Listen to people talking about things they did this year. Number the things they talk about from 1–6.

Part 2 Listen again. Did they have positive or negative feelings about what they did? Write **+** for positive or **✗** for negative.

	Number	Feeling
Went overseas		
Bought something expensive		
Met someone		
Moved to a new house		
Changed schools		
Studied something new		

Part 3 Talk with a partner. Who had the best year? Who had the worst year?

LET'S TALK

Part 1 Did you do any of the things below recently? Check (✔) the things you did.

Part 2 Ask your partner the questions. Ask for more information, and write it in the chart. Reverse roles.

	When was the last time you...?	Follow-up questions
1	read a good book	What did you read?
2	saw a terrific movie	What movie did you see?
3	went to a live concert	Who did you see?
4	went to a great party	Where did you go?
5	went out to dinner	Who with?
6	met someone special	Who did you meet?
7	bought something special	What did you buy?

Part 3 Did you and your partner have anything in common? Report to the class.

Conversation 2

What are your plans?

What plans do you have for the next 12 months?

Class CD 2, Track 59

Yi-lin: So what are your plans for next year, Rina? Are you going to get a job?
Rina: No, I'm going to go to college.
Yi-lin: Great. What school are you going to go to?
Rina: I want to go to City College. Lots of my friends are going there.
Yi-lin: Oh. So what do you want to study?
Rina: I want to study business.
Yi-lin: That's interesting.
Rina: Yeah, I want to open a business after I graduate.
Yi-lin: Well, good luck.

Class CD 2, Track 60
Pronunciation Focus

Notice how *want to* is pronounced in these sentences.

I want to go to City College.
What do you want to study?
I want to study business.

Listen to the conversation again and notice the pronunciation of *want to*.

1. Talking about future plans

What are you	going to do next year?	I'm going to go to college.
What is he / she		He's / She's going to get a job.
What are they		They're going to get married.
Are you going to	go to college?	Yes, I am.
	travel?	No, I'm going to get a job.
		No, I'm not going to.

PRACTICE 1

Class CD 2
Track 61

Listen to the example. What are you going to do at the times below? Why? Complete the chart with information about yourself. Use the suggestions or your own information. Then compare with a partner.

		You	**Your partner**
1	after this class		
2	next semester		
3	next year		
4	next summer		
5	next vacation		

Use These Words

get a part-time job
stay home
study
take a break
take a trip somewhere
I'm not sure
take a vacation

PRACTICE 2

Work with a different partner. Tell him or her about your partner's plans in Practice 1.

A: After this class, David is going to take up jogging.
B: Why is he going to do that?
A: He wants to get in shape.

2. Talking about wants

What do you want to do?	I want to	get a job.
		open a business.
	I don't want to study.	
Do you want to	get a job?	Yes, I do.
	travel?	No, not really.

PRACTICE 1

Class CD 2 Track 62

Listen to the example. Check (✓) the things you want to do in the next 12 months. Then ask your partner questions. Reverse roles.

1. __ travel overseas
2. __ get a job
3. __ change jobs
4. __ take another English course
5. __ have more fun

6. __ go to university
7. __ get a boyfriend/girlfriend
8. __ get engaged
9. __ get married
10. __ buy a car

A: What do you want to do?
B: Well, I want to…
A: Do you want to…?

PRACTICE 2

Class CD 2 Track 63

Listen to the example. Complete the chart with your answers. Then ask a partner the questions. Reverse roles.

1	What place do you want to visit sometime?	
2	What is a sport you want to try?	
3	What is something you want to buy?	
4	Who is someone famous you want to meet?	

LISTEN TO THIS

Class CD 2 Track 64

Part 1 Listen to Robert talking about things he is thinking of doing next year. Check (✓) the things he plans to do.

Part 2 Listen again. Why does he want to do these things? Write his reasons in the chart.

		Yes	Why?/Why not?
1	learn Spanish		
2	teach English		
3	take a photography class		

Part 3 Talk with a partner. Do you want to do any of these things?

Part 1 Interview your partner and ask these questions. Take notes.

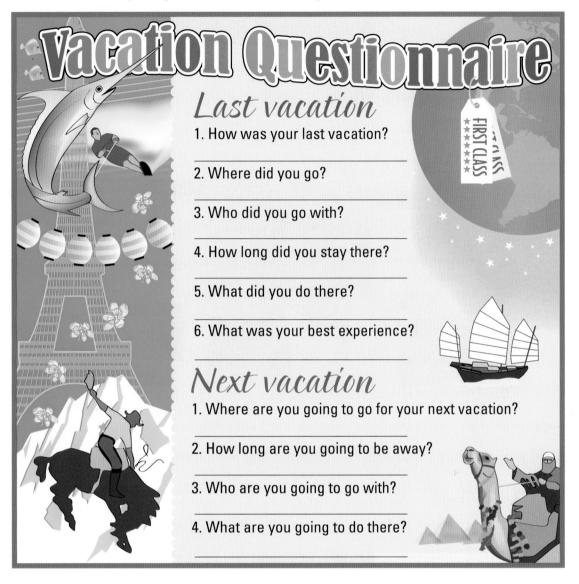

Vacation Questionnaire

Last vacation

1. How was your last vacation?

2. Where did you go?

3. Who did you go with?

4. How long did you stay there?

5. What did you do there?

6. What was your best experience?

Next vacation

1. Where are you going to go for your next vacation?

2. How long are you going to be away?

3. Who are you going to go with?

4. What are you going to do there?

Part 2 Reverse roles.

Part 3 Get together with another pair and share your information in groups.

1. Who had…
   the best vacation?
   the most interesting vacation experience?
2. Who has…
   the most interesting vacation plans?

Now Try This

In your groups, plan a five-day vacation for a visitor to your country. Suggest places for them to visit, how long to spend there, and what to do. Then compare your plans with others.

LISTEN TO THIS   UNIT 10

Class CD 2
Track 65

Part 1 Listen to people giving directions. Number the places on the map from 1–6.

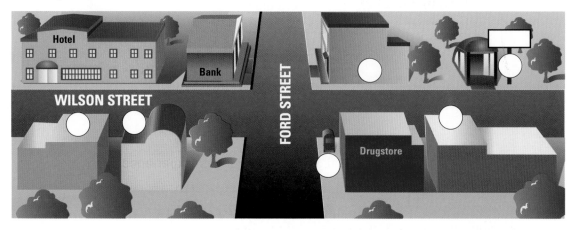

Part 2 Ask your partner questions to find out if your answers are the same.

GIVE IT A TRY

Talk with your partner about places in your neighborhood.

hairdresser   cafe   bank   fast-food restaurant   park   post office

1. Are the places above in your neighborhood?
2. Which of them do you visit regularly?
3. Tell your partner how to get to these places.
4. What other places do you go to in your neighborhood?

LISTEN TO THIS   UNIT 11

Class CD 2
Track 66

Part 1 Listen to four short conversations. Does Speaker 1 ask for permission to do something or ask to borrow something? Write a check (✓) in the correct column.

	Permission	Borrow	Agrees	Doesn't agree
1				
2				
3				
4				

Part 2 Listen again. Does Speaker 2 agree or not agree to the request? Write a check (✔) in the correct column.

GIVE IT A TRY

You are on vacation with a friend. Your partner will ask to borrow things from you. Think of reasons for saying no to these requests. Reverse roles.

1. Could I use your toothbrush? I forgot to bring one.
2. Can you lend me a shirt? I didn't bring enough clothes with me.
3. Is it all right if I make a few calls on your cell phone?
4. I'm running out of money. Can I borrow a couple of hundred dollars from you?
5. Can I borrow your sunglasses? They look really cool.
6. Do you mind if I use your digital camera? I forgot to bring mine.

LISTEN TO THIS   UNIT 12

**Class CD 2
Track 67** Jo is talking about her summer plans. Check (✔) if these statements are *true* or *false*.

	True	False
1. She's going to go away next summer.	☐	☐
2. She's not going to work while she is there.	☐	☐
3. She is going to go with a friend.	☐	☐
4. She is going to stay in hostels.	☐	☐
5. She is going to be away for a year.	☐	☐

GIVE IT A TRY

Work in groups. What do you want to do in the future? Talk with your group. Use the questions below to start, and ask follow-up questions.

1. How many people in your group want to:
   travel (where)?
   study (what)?
   work (doing what)?
   buy a car?
   your idea? _____

2. What do you need to do in order to achieve your plans? Ask your partners. Switch roles.

(Students C and D look at this page. Students A and B look at page 9.)

Part 1 Student C, introduce yourself to Student D. Write your information below. Reverse roles.

Student C

Mr./Ms./Mrs./Miss
First name: _____
Last name: _____

Student D

Mr./Ms./Mrs./Miss
First name: _____
Last name: _____

Part 2 Work in groups. Introduce your partner to the other people in your group. Switch roles. Write their information below.

Student A

Mr./Ms./Mrs./Miss
First name: _____
Last name: _____

Student B

Mr./Ms./Mrs./Miss
First name: _____
Last name: _____

Now Try This

Get together with a different of students. Introduce your partner and ask about your classmates.

(Student B looks at this page. Student A looks at page 17.)

Part 1 Look at the things in the picture. Compare your picture with your partner's picture. How many differences can you find?

A: Do you have a camera in your picture?
B: Yes, I do.
A: Where is it?
B: It's on the table.
A: In my picture it's…

Part 2 Work with a different partner and compare your differences.

Example: I have six differences. In my picture, the camera is on the table. In my partner's picture the camera is…

Now Try This

Work with a partner. Write six statements about things in the classroom. Two of them are false. Then join another pair of students. Read your statements. Your partners say if the statements are true or false. Reverse roles.

(Student B looks at this page. Student A looks at page 25.)

Part 1 Look at the photos of Salina and Brendan. Answer your partner's questions about them.

Salina

22 years old

150 centimeters

1 sister, no brothers

Mother: teacher;

Father: business person

Interests: action movies;

sports, especially tennis;

reading

Brendan

25 years old

180 centimeters

3 sisters, 2 brothers

Mother: doctor;

Father: engineer

Interests: comedies

(movies); education;

soccer

Part 2 What does Salina do? What does Brendan do? Tell your partner what you think.

Part 3 Look at the photos of Pelisa and Trent. Your partner has information about them. You will ask your partner questions about them.

Pelisa

Trent

Write the questions you will ask to find out their age, height, family, and interests.

1. _____?

2. _____?

3. _____?

4. _____?

5. your idea: _____?

Part 4 What does Trent do? What does Pelisa do? Tell your partner what you think.

Now Try This

Imagine you are going to interview a celebrity. Who will you interview? What questions will you ask? Make a list.

(Student B looks at this page. Student A looks at page 35.)

Part 1 Look at the picture. You are at a party. Your partner is going to ask you about one person in the picture below.

Part 2 Listen to the description of your partner's friend. Say where he is.

Part 3 Now you are looking for a friend at the party. Look at the picture of your friend. What does she look like? What is she wearing? Tell your partner.

Gita

Now Try This

Think of unusual clothing you have seen recently (e.g., in a magazine, on television, or on the street). Describe it to your partner.

(Student B looks at this page. Student A looks at page 69.)

Part 1 You are working in a cafe. A customer wants to know what is on the menu for breakfast. Answer his or her questions.

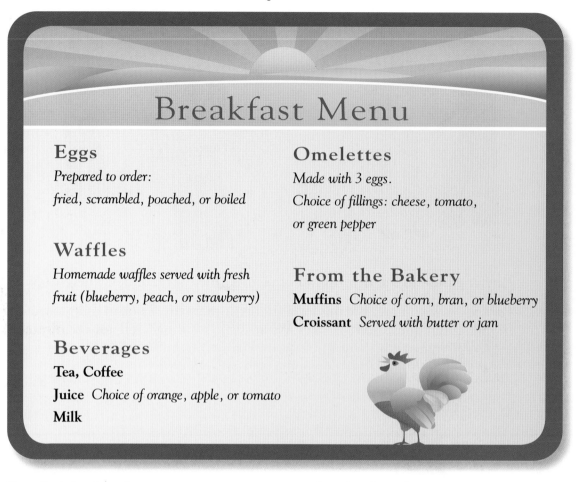

Breakfast Menu

Eggs
Prepared to order:
fried, scrambled, poached, or boiled

Waffles
Homemade waffles served with fresh fruit (blueberry, peach, or strawberry)

Beverages
Tea, Coffee
Juice *Choice of orange, apple, or tomato*
Milk

Omelettes
Made with 3 eggs.
Choice of fillings: cheese, tomato, or green pepper

From the Bakery
Muffins *Choice of corn, bran, or blueberry*
Croissant *Served with butter or jam*

Part 2 Ask what the customer wants to eat and to drink. Take notes.

Part 3 Reverse roles. You are the customer, and your partner is the server. Decide what you want to eat and drink and tell your partner.

Now Try This

Work with your partner. Prepare a simple breakfast menu for a cafe in your country. Then use your menu and role-play ordering breakfast.

(Student B looks at this page. Student A looks at page 77.)

Part 1 You are interested in applying for one of the jobs below. Decide which one you think you are most qualified for.

Summer Jobs Available

Reporter for college magazine

Baby-sitter on cruise ship

Part 2 Your partner will ask you about your skills. Answer the questions and find out which job is best for you.

Part 3 Look at these two ads for summer jobs. What special skills or abilities do you think a person would need for each job? Choose from the box and add your own ideas. Write *S* next to the skills a sales assistant needs. Write *T* next to the skills a telemarketer needs.

Summer Jobs Available

Sales assistant in music store

Telephone-marketing salesperson for health foods

good at languages ___	flexible ___
good at English ___	persuasive ___
a good communicator ___	good IT skills ___
good at sports ___	good sense of humor ___
creative ___	sings well ___
patient ___	plays a musical instrument ___
your idea _____	your idea _____

Part 4 Your partner is interested in applying for one of the jobs above. Ask about his or her skills. Tell your partner which job you think is best for him or her.

Now Try This

What hobbies and pastimes do people enjoy that are special to your country? Do they require any special skills or abilities?

(Student B looks at this page. Student A looks at page 87.)

Part 1 Look at your map. Your partner is new in town. Answer his or her questions. You are both at **✗**.

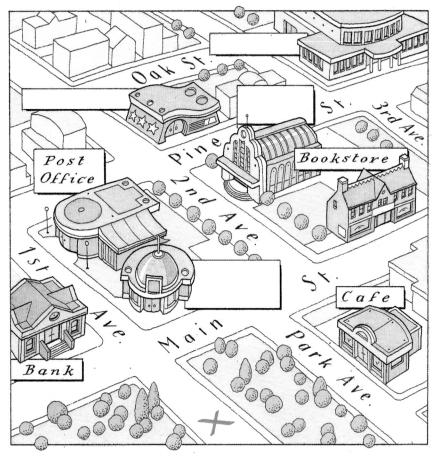

Part 2 Ask your partner about these places: a nightclub, a school, a tourist information center, a movie theater. Label them on your map.

Part 3 Add these places to your map: a hairdresser, a travel agency, a museum. Answer your partner's questions about how to get to each place.

(Student B looks at this page. Student A looks at page 95.)

Part 1 Your roommate wants to borrow three things from you. Agree to lend one but not the others. Give a reason for saying no.

Part 2 Ask your roommate's permission to do the things below. Check (✔) the thing he or she agrees to and write the excuses he or she offers for the others.

		Agrees	Doesn't agree	Excuse
1	rearrange the furniture in the apartment			
2	lend the TV to a friend			
3	get a puppy			

Part 3 Change partners. This time you are Student A.

Now Try This

Someone wants to borrow money, your tennis racket, and your magazine. Think of excuses for not lending these items.

Audio script

Unit 1

GIVE IT A TRY   **PAGE 3**

1. Introducing yourself

PRACTICE 1

A: Hello. My name's Robert. But please call me Bob.

PRACTICE 2

A: My name is Tracy Park. My first name is Tracy. My last name is Park. Please call me Tracy.

2. Greeting people

1

A: Hi, Bob.

B: Hi, Eun-mi.

A: How are you today?

B: Fine, thanks. How are you?

A: Good, thanks.

2

C: Good morning.

D: Hello, Mr. Stevens.

3. Saying good-bye

1

A: OK. See you later.

B: Yeah, see you.

2

A: Well, nice talking to you. Good-bye.

B: Good-bye.

LISTEN TO THIS   **PAGE 5**

1

W: Hi, Cheng-han. How are things?

C: Pretty good, thanks. And you?

W: Fine, thanks. How was your weekend?

C: Great, thanks. How about you?

W: It was OK. Oh, it's time for class. See you.

C: Yeah. Have a nice day.

2

S: Hey, Jean. Good to see you again.

J: Hi, Simon. How are things?

S: Good, thanks. How are you?

J: Fine, thanks.

S: Are you going downtown?

J: Yes, I am. Bye.

S: Bye-bye.

3

B: Good evening. I'm Brian Baxter.

T: Hello. I'm Ted Ozaki.

B: Nice to meet you, Ted.

T: Are you from the States?

B: No, I'm Canadian, from Toronto.

T: That's a great city.

B: Yeah. Well, nice talking to you.

T: See you again.

4

P: Hello. My name's Pei-ling.

M: Nice to meet you.

P: Say, are you in my Spanish class?

M: No, I'm taking Korean.

P: Oh, yeah? Class starts at 11, doesn't it?

M: That's right. See you later.

GIVE IT A TRY   **PAGE 7**

1. Finding out about people

A: Who's that guy?

B: That's Tony. Who's she?

A: That's Nishi.

2. Introducing people

A: Tony, this is my friend, Nishi.

B: Hi, Nishi. Nice to meet you.

C: Hi. Nice to meet you, too.

LISTEN TO THIS   **PAGE 8**

1

M: Who's that guy?

P: Oh, that's Johnny Chen. He's a good friend of mine. Don't you know him?

M: No, I don't.

P: Really? Hey, Johnny!

J: Hi, guys.

P: Johnny. This is Maya.

J: Hi, Maya. Nice to meet you.

M: Nice to meet you, too.

2

M: Who's that woman with the red hair?

P: That's Sandra.

M: Is she in your class?

P: No, she's my neighbor.

M: Really?

P: Yeah. Let me introduce you. She's really nice.

M: OK.

P: Oh, Sandra. This is Maya.

S: Hi, Maya. Nice to meet you.

M: Yeah, you too.

3

M: Who's that man?

P: Oh, that's my Japanese teacher, Mr. Okano.

M: Really. Is he from Tokyo?

P: No, he's from Sapporo. Let's talk to him. Good morning, Mr. Okano.

O: *Ohayō gozaimasu*, Phillip.

P: Mr. Okano. I'd like you to meet my friend Maya.

O: Hello, Maya. Nice to meet you.

M: Nice to meet you, too.

4

M: Is that one of your teachers?

P: No, she's in my computer class. She's really nice. Do you want to meet her?

M: Sure.

P: Oh, Ms. Ford. I'd like you to meet my friend Maya.

F: How do you do?

M: Nice to meet you.

Unit 2

GIVE IT A TRY   **PAGE 11**

1. Identifying things (1)

A: What's this?

B: It's my cell phone.

A: What are these?

B: They're earrings.

2. Identifying things (2)

A: Whose earrings are these?

B: They're Karen's.

3. Complimenting people

A: Hi, Jim.

B: Hi, Kumiko.

A: How are things?

B: Pretty good, thanks.

A: Oh, I like your T-shirt. It's cool.

B: Thanks. And that's a nice watch.

A: Thanks. Well, see you later.

B: Bye.

LISTEN TO THIS   **PAGE 13**

S: Hey, Amanda. Could you help me sort the clothes?

A: Sure. Are these your socks, Suzie?

S: Yeah, they're mine. Thanks.

A: What about these jeans? Are they yours or mine?

S: Let me see. Oh, they're too small for me. They're yours.

A: OK. And this T-shirt is mine, too. But I think this top is yours. Take a look.

S: Yep. That's mine.

A: Pass me the dress. That's mine. But not the shorts.

S: Yeah, they're mine. But not the scarf. Here.

A: Thanks.

S: That's funny. Where are my pants?

A: Hmm… They're not here. And I can't find my gloves or my jacket.

S: Oh, here's your jacket. But your gloves aren't here.

. **Describing where things are**
: Where are my keys?
: They're in the bedroom.
: Where's my book?
: It's next to the sofa.

. **Asking where things are**
: Is the newspaper on the table?
: Yes, it is.
: Are the magazines on the sofa?
: No, they aren't. They're on the table.

: I'm looking for my cell phone.
: It's over there, on top of the bookshelf.
: Right. And what about my camera?
: Look. There it is. On top of the TV. And your wallet is next to the TV if you're looking for it.
: Of course.
: Where are those magazines I was reading, by the way?
: Oh, I put them in the drawer.
: OK. And my watch is here, too. But my sunglasses… Did you see them?
: Yeah. They're on the floor, next to the sofa. See?
: Oh, yeah.
: And where are my shoes?
: There, in front of the bookshelf.
: OK. And where did I put my briefcase?
: It's under the table.
: What about the remote control?
: It's on the sofa.
: And one more thing. Where is my tennis racket?
: It's behind the door.

nit 3

. **Describing personal information**
: How old are you?
: I'm 18.
: How tall are you?
: I'm 172 centimeters tall.

2. **Talking about interests (1)**
: Are you interested in sports?
: Sure.
: What kind of sports are you interested in?
: I like swimming.

3. **Talking about interests (2)**
: Are you interested in movies?
: Yeah.
: What kind?
: I like comedies.

1
: What are you doing on Saturday, David?
: I want to watch the school baseball game. I love baseball.

A: Me too. What other sports do you like?
D: Tennis is my other favorite sport.
A: And do you play basketball?
D: Sure.
A: I thought so. You are really tall. How tall are you?
D: I'm 178 cms.
A: Wow. And you're only 14 years old!

2
A: Are you going to join the drama club this semester, Meena?
M: I don't think so. I want to play more sports. I'm going to join the sports club.
A: Great. What sports do you like?
M: Volleyball and basketball. I'm kind of short for both games, but it doesn't matter. I love them.
A: So how tall are you?
M: 169 cm.
A: And how old are you?
M: Nineteen.

3
A: Are you going to play baseball on Saturday, Sandra?
S: No, I need some new sneakers. I'm going downtown to look for some. I also need a new tennis racket.
A: So you're good at baseball *and* tennis? Fantastic! And you're only 18.
S: I also play volleyball.
A: Wow! Are you the tallest person on the team?
S: No, I'm 180 cm, but Julia is 187 cm.

1. **Talking about family members**
A: Tell me about Sam's family.
B: He comes from a medium-sized family.
A: How many brothers and sisters does he have?
B: He has two brothers.

2. **Asking about family members**
A: What do your parents do?
B: My father is an engineer and my mother is a pharmacist.
A: How old are they?
B: My father is 44, and my mother is 42.
A: What are their names?
B: My dad's name is John and my mother's name is Karen.

F: So tell me about your family, Michelle.
M: OK. Well, there are five people in my family. My mom is 42, and she has a small export business.
F: That's interesting. What does she export?
M: She exports furniture.
F: I see.
M: And I have one sister, Su-Jun. She's younger than me. She's 15. She's very good at music and plays the piano and the violin.
F: How nice! And what about your dad? What does he do?

M: He's a dentist. He's 44 and he studied in Canada.
F: Really? And do you have any brothers?
M: Yes, I have one older brother and one younger one. My older brother is 20, and my younger brother is 11. They're both crazy about soccer.
F: And what about you? Are you too?
M: No, not really.

Review Unit 1

R: Who's that over there, Paul?
P: Her name's Taylor.
R: She's pretty.
P: Yes, she is. She's my dance teacher.
R: Oh, are you taking dance lessons, Paul?
P: Yes, I am. Taylor's a very good dancer.
R: Really? Is Taylor her last name?
P: No, it's her first name. Her last name's Johnson.
R: Nice name. Taylor Johnson.
P: Yes, it is. Do you want to meet her?
R: Sure!
P: OK. [pause] Oh, Taylor, this is my friend Robert.
T: Hello, Robert. Nice to meet you.
R: Hi. Nice to meet you, too.

Review Unit 2

A: Oh, no! I broke my glasses, and I can't see a thing without them.
B: What are you looking for?
A: Well, where's my bag? I thought I put it on the table last night.
B: It's right there—in front of the table.
A: OK. And it looks like it's going to rain. I'll need my umbrella when I go out. I usually put it under the table.
B: No, it's not under the table. Look there, behind the table on the left. Do you see it?
A: Oh, right. Thanks. And where did I put my notebook?
B: Umm… I saw it somewhere a few minutes ago.
A: Is it on the table?
B: No. Let me look in the drawer. Yes, it's in here. And are you looking for your watch, too?
A: Yes, I thought it was in the drawer, too.
B: No, it isn't. It's on the table near the back.
A: Oh, yeah. And I wonder where I put my cell phone.
B: There it is. Under the table.
A: How did it get there? Oh, and one more thing. Where's today's paper?
B: There it is, on the floor next to the table.

Review Unit 3

LISTEN TO THIS   PAGE 27

M-J: What do you like to do in your free time, Rod?

R: Well, Min-joo, I'm into music, so I play guitar. I really love rock music. Do you like rock music?

M-J: Not really. I'm more interested in classical music. I play the piano and listen to a lot of piano music.

R: Are you interested in sports?

M-J: Not so much. But I love reading. I really like detective stories.

R: Oh, cool. How about you, Tina? Do you like music?

T: No, not really. I'm more into sports.

R: What kind of sports are you interested in?

T: I love tennis and basketball. And I also enjoy traveling. How about you, James? What are you interested in?

J: Actually, I really like traveling. I want to be a tour guide some day.

T: Really? Where do you like to travel?

J: Oh, everywhere, but I'm really interested in Asia—especially Thailand and Singapore.

T: OK. What else are you interested in? Do you like music?

J: Yes, I do. Especially rock.

M-J: So that leaves you, Kazu. What do you like to do in your free time?

K: Hmm. I guess traveling is something I love. I also like all kinds of sports. Especially surfing and swimming.

Unit 4

GIVE IT A TRY   PAGE 29

1. Describing colors and clothing

A: What colors are you wearing today?

B: My shirt is red. My shoes are dark blue.

2. Describing people

A: What does Sandy look like?

B: She's medium height. She's wearing brown pants and a red shirt.

LISTEN TO THIS   PAGE 31

1. He is medium height. He has curly hair and wears glasses. He likes bright colors.
2. She's pretty short. She likes to wear her hair short. She wears glasses and today she's wearing pants. She and Anne are best friends.
3. She's very tall. She has long blond hair and she's wearing a jacket and pants today. She is Ted's sister.
4. He has long hair and is medium height, I guess. He often wears shorts and a cap.
5. He's medium height, and a little heavy. He has short blond hair and likes to wear T-shirts and shorts. He is Bill's brother.

GIVE IT A TRY   PAGE 33

1. Giving opinions

A: How do you like these shoes?

B: They're great.

2. Talking about prices

A: How much is the watch?

B: It's $55.00.

A: That's not bad.

LISTEN TO THIS   PAGE 34

1

D: How do you like this phone?

J: Hmm. I like it a lot. It's very small, isn't it? And it's very light, too.

D: The screen is really sharp.

J: I'd love to get one. But how much is it?

D: It's $350.00.

J: Oh, that's too much for me. Let's try to find a cheaper one.

2

D: Hey, look at these shoes. What do you think of them?

J: I don't really like them. I don't like the design.

D: Yeah. They don't really look very nice. And look at the price—$199.00—way too expensive!

J: Yeah.

3

J: Are you looking for a new watch? Take a look at this one. What do you think?

D: It's not bad.

J: Yeah, it looks OK. But the price is really good. It's only $20.00.

D: That's cheap. I think I'll get it. I really need a new one.

4

J: Why don't you try on these sunglasses? I think they're really cool.

D: Let me see. Yeah…very cool!

J: And they're on sale. They're only $29.95.

D: That's not bad. I'll buy them. They'll be great for the beach.

Unit 5

GIVE IT A TRY   PAGE 37

1. Telling the time

PRACTICE 1

A: It's 10:00.

B: It's 10:05.

PRACTICE 2

A: What time is it?

B: It's 8:30.

2. Talking about routines

A: What time do you get up?

B: I usually get up at 6:30. What time do you get up?

LISTEN TO THIS   PAGE 39

1

I: So you're a hair stylist, Chris?

C: That's right.

I: What's your job like?

C: It's great. I meet all kinds of interesting people. Last week an actor from that new TV soap opera came in for a cut.

I: Is that right? And do you work long hours?

C: Lots of my clients are working people and they like to come in after work. So I start at 2:00 in the afternoon and finish at 10:00 at night.

2

I: So, Kayla, what does a dog walker do exactly?

K: I walk dogs, of course! I go to people's apartments, pick up their dogs, and take them for a walk. I walk six dogs at a time and walk them for two or three hours. Then I take them back and pick up another group of dogs and take them for a walk, too. Usually I start around 9:00 A.M. and finish at 4:00 in the afternoon.

I: And how do you like it?

K: I love it. I love dogs, and I love working outdoors so it's perfect for me.

3

I: Where are you working at the moment, Tim?

T: I'm working at the ticket office at the Verona Cinema.

I: Oh, yeah?

T: But I want to change jobs. The work is boring, the hours are really long, and the money isn't good.

I: What hours do you work?

T: I start at 10:30 A.M. We show the first movie of the day at 11:00. Then we often have late movies, and I have to be there until pretty late—usually until midnight.

I: Wow! That's a long day. No wonder you're looking for a new job.

4

I: What do you do, Celia?

C: I teach ballet.

I: That's interesting.

C: Yeah, I have my own studio. I don't dance professionally much anymore, so it's nice to be teaching ballet. I love it, and I have some great students.

I: Do you teach every day?

C: Not on Sunday, but I teach every other day. Most of my students come after school so I start at 3:00 in the afternoon. My last class is at 8:00 P.M. and I finish at 10:00. I'm really tired at the end of the day.

I: Yeah, I'm sure you are.

1. Talking about the week

Monday
Tuesday
Wednesday
Thursday
Friday
Saturday
Sunday

2. Talking about activities

A: Do you have classes on Friday?
B: No, I don't.
A: What do you do on Friday nights?
B: I go out with my friends.

H: Are you busy this week, Paul? When can we get together to see a movie or something?
P: Let me check. OK. So I'm going ice-skating with Kelly on Monday at 4:00 P.M. I guess we'll be there until dinnertime and then go off together. So Monday's not good. On Tuesday I have a guitar lesson at 5:00 P.M. It only lasts an hour so I'm free after that.
H: Tuesday's not good for me. I have a Spanish class that starts at 6:00.
P: Thursday I need to make an appointment to see the doctor. And Suzie's birthday party is on Friday night at 8:00 so Friday's not good for me.
H: How about Saturday?
P: Hmm...I'm not sure about Saturday. I want to see the dentist, and I want to make an appointment some time on Saturday morning. And Saturday afternoon I'm meeting Terry and Pat for coffee at 2:30.
H: OK. So it looks like Wednesday night is good for you?
P: Sure. Wednesday looks good.

Unit 6

1. Talking about school

A: What does Emi do?
B: She's a college student.
A: Where is she studying?
B: She goes to City College.
A: What is she studying?
B: She's majoring in fashion design.

2. Giving an opinion about school and study

A: How do you like your school?
B: It's OK.
A: And how do you like your classes?
B: I like them a lot.

1

I: Where are you going to school, Martin?
M: I'm a freshman at City University.
I: Uh-huh. I hear it's a very good university.
M: Yes, it is. I'm really happy there.
I: Are you studying fine arts?
M: No, I am studying IT.
I: I see. And how do you like your classes?
M: They're OK. Some are kind of difficult, but the professors are really good.

2

I: Where are you studying, Rosie?
R: I'm still at the local junior college. It's really boring. But I'm hoping to go to the university next semester.
I: What are you studying?
R: I'm doing a general liberal arts course.
I: Do you have a major?
R: Yes, I'm studying American literature. But it's not very interesting. I haven't learned anything new all year.

3

I: What are you studying, Liz?
L: I'm majoring in music.
I: Great. That must be very interesting.
L: Yes, it is. I love it. And I have great teachers. Some of them are pretty famous musicians.
I: Wonderful. And where are you studying?
L: I'm at the national university. I love it!

1. Talking about personal qualities

A: I think fun is a positive quality.
B: I agree.
A: I think talkative is a negative quality. What do you think?

2. Comparing personal qualities

A: Who is your best friend?
B: My best friend is my sister, Anna.
A: How similar are you?
B: Well, we are both talkative.
A: And how are you different?

W: How is everything at college, Colin?
C: Pretty good.
W: Do you like the dormitory?
C: Yes. My roommate is from Brazil.
W: Oh, yeah. What's he like?
C: Well, he's really friendly. He's always meeting new people. And he has a great sense of humor. He always makes me laugh.
W: That's nice.
C: Yeah. He's a very good student and studies very hard. And he's kind of interesting, too. He likes insects and is always coming back with some strange insect he found somewhere. And he has two big black spiders as pets. He keeps them in a big jar next to his bed.

W: That sounds a little creepy.
C: Oh, I don't mind. I wish he would keep his part of the room a little cleaner though. He leaves things on the floor all the time.
W: Is that right?
C: And he's pretty forgetful, too. Sometimes he says he wants to meet me for lunch in the cafeteria but half the time he forgets and never shows up.
W: Oh, dear. That's too bad.

Review Unit 4

B: Hi, Kim. I'm at immigration now. I won't be long.
K: Great. I'm waiting in the meeting area.
B: I don't know what you look like. How tall are you?
K: Uh, well I'm pretty tall. Are you tall or short?
B: I guess I'm medium height.
K: And I have short brown hair. How about you?
B: I have black hair.
K: Are you wearing glasses?
B: No, I'm not. Are you?
K: Yes, I am.
B: OK. And what are you wearing? I'm wearing brown pants and a blue shirt.
K: I'm wearing blue jeans and a yellow top.
B: Great. So I'll see you in a few minutes.
K: Yeah. I'm sure I can find you.

Review Unit 5

A: So why don't we try to meet for dinner some time this week?
D: That would be great. But I have a pretty busy week. How about you?
A: Me too. But let's see if we can find a day when we're both free.
D: Well, I can't do it tonight. I have a math class until 9:00 P.M. on Mondays.
A: Yuck. Anyway, I'm not free tonight either.
D: That's too bad. Now let's see. How does Tuesday look for you? It's OK for me.
A: Let me think. Oh, I can't do Tuesday. I have a driving lesson. And Wednesday night, my sister and I always go to the gym.
D: Wednesday's not good for me either because I have a basketball game.
A: Hey, this is getting difficult. What else have I got on this week? Oh, yes. I have a meeting I have to go to on Friday. The weekend I am not free at all because I promised to meet friends on both Saturday and Sunday.
D: So where does that leave us? I don't have anything else planned for this week.

Review Unit 6

LISTEN TO THIS   PAGE 53

A: I think for a roommate, you want someone who is really considerate—someone who doesn't only think about themselves. They think about the other person, you know, so they don't have the TV on when the other person is sleeping, that kind of thing.

B: Right. And I like someone who keeps the place clean—they don't leave their clothes all over the room and stuff like that.

A: And it's also good if they know how to do things, like cooking, and fixing things that go wrong, or even if they know how to change a lightbulb.

B: Yes. It's great if a roommate is practical like that. How about good qualities for a travel companion?

A: Well, a travel companion should be practical, too. And you want someone to keep you company. They should be friendly and talkative.

B: Right. And someone who likes meeting people and who is outgoing. Because it's nice to get to meet people when you're traveling. Otherwise, what's the point of leaving home?

A: And if you're going to spend a lot of time together, you want someone who is easy to get along with. They don't lose their temper or get stressed out.

B: Right. They should be relaxed and friendly.

Unit 7

GIVE IT A TRY   PAGE 55

1. Talking about routines (1)

PRACTICE 1

A: What do you usually do on Saturday morning?

B: I usually surf the web and sometimes I play sports. What about you?

A: Saturday morning? I always sleep in!

PRACTICE 2

A: What do you usually do in the morning?

B: I usually get up early in the morning.

A: What about in the afternoon?

B: I often play soccer in the afternoon.

2. Talking about routines (2)

A: Do you ever play sports on the weekend?

B: Yes, I sometimes play tennis. Do you ever play sports on the weekend?

A: No, not very often.

LISTEN TO THIS   PAGE 57

I: Wow. You're a model! That must be exciting!

A: It's a lot of fun. I love it. But sometimes it's very tiring.

I: Tiring? Why is that?

A: Well I often have all-day shoots on Saturdays, and have to get up very early. I usually get up around 5:00 A.M., and then a car from the studio comes to pick me up at 6:00 and take me to the location.

I: Does it take a long time to shoot the photos?

A: Sometimes. The other models and I often have to change clothes ten or more times. And it takes about an hour to take all the photos with each set of clothes. So I often spend 10 or 12 hours on a photo shoot.

I: I see.

A: So I get home pretty late, and when I do, I'm really tired and hungry.

I: I bet! And what about the clothes you model? Do you get to keep them?

A: Unfortunately not! But the work pays really well. I sometimes make five or six hundred dollars for one day.

I: That's pretty good. And do you work on Sundays, too?

A: Not usually. But on Sundays I spend about four hours in the gym working out to keep in shape.

I: So I guess you don't have time to see a movie next weekend?

A: No, I'm sorry. But thanks for asking

GIVE IT A TRY   PAGE 59

1. Asking about the weekend

A: Hi, Paul. How was your weekend?

B: It was OK thanks. How was yours?

A: It was very quiet—nice and relaxing.

B: That sounds good.

2. Talking about past events (1)

A: What did you do on the weekend?

B: I visited friends. What did you do?

A: I went to the beach.

3. Talking about past events (2)

A: Did you have a nice weekend?

B: Yes, I did.

A: Did you go the movies?

B: No, I didn't. I went shopping. I bought some great CDs.

LISTEN TO THIS   PAGE 60

S: How was your weekend, Tamika?

T: Pretty good, thanks.

S: Did you go to the rock concert in the park?

T: No, I didn't. Did you?

S: No, I didn't either. But I heard it was terrific.

T: Yeah, I heard it was fabulous. I saw a great movie though.

S: Oh, me too. What did you see?

T: I saw that new Tom Cruise movie. It's really good.

S: Oh, good. I'm going to see it this weekend. I saw a Korean movie on Friday night. It was pretty good. Then after the movie I went to a club with some friends.

T: Oh, yeah? And did you go to Janet's party on Saturday night?

S: I wanted to, but I decided to study for my economics test.

T: You are such a good student! I didn't go to the party either because it was my dad's birthday. We went out for a family dinner. Sunday was fun though because I played a great game of soccer.

S: I didn't know you played soccer!

T: Yeah, I do. It's fun. Did you get to play sports at all over the weekend?

S: I wanted to, but I had a lot of things to do around the house.

T: Too bad. I hate housework.

S: Yeah, so do I.

Unit 8

GIVE IT A TRY   PAGE 63

1. Asking about meals

A: What do you have for breakfast?

B: I usually have toast and fruit. What about you?

A: I usually have rice and eggs. And what do you have to drink?

B: I usually have coffee.

2. Asking about likes

A: Do you like coffee?

B: Not really. What about you?

A: Yes, I do.

LISTEN TO THIS   PAGE 65

R: Hi, Aran. Hey, I'm really hungry. I'm going to have a big breakfast today.

A: Me too, Robert.

R: What do people usually have for breakfast in Thailand, Aran?

A: Well we don't really have a special meal for breakfast, like you do in many countries. We usually just have something that we cooked the night before for supper, you know, so there will always be rice of course, and usually some vegetable dish, and then maybe a curry dish, like curried chicken or beef. And tea or coffee to drink.

R: Mmm. Sounds delicious.

A: Yeah, but I usually just have a western breakfast—you know toast, coffee, and some fruit. How about in the UK?

R: Well a typical English breakfast—that's difficult—it depends on what part of the country you live in, but I guess I can say people will have fried eggs, sausages, bacon, fried mushrooms, and tomatoes—everything fried so it's rather heavy. And tea with toast.

A: So is that what you have?

R: No. I have two boiled eggs, cereal, and juice.

A: Very healthy!

GIVE IT A TRY   PAGE 67

. Asking about wants and preferences

PRACTICE 1

.: Are you hungry?

.: Yes, I am.

.: What do you feel like?

.: Maybe a milk shake.

PRACTICE 2

.: Would you like something to eat?

.: No, not right now.

.: Would you like something to drink?

.: Yes, please. I'd like a milk shake.

LISTEN TO THIS   PAGE 68

: Are you ready to order?

M: Yes, I'd like a chicken salad, please.

: Sure. And would you like bread with that?

M: OK.

: What kind of dressing would you like?

M: I'll have Italian. And for dessert I'd like a slice of chocolate cake.

: Fine. Would you like anything to drink?

M: Yes. I'd like iced coffee, please.

: With cream?

M: No, black please and plenty of ice.

: Certainly. And how about you, sir?

: I'll have the club sandwich, please.

: And would you like french fries with that?

: Yes, please.

: Anything else?

: I'd like juice. What kind of juices do you have?

: We have orange, tomato, apple, and grapefruit.

: I'd like apple juice please, but with no ice, please.

: OK. Thank you.

Unit 9

GIVE IT A TRY   PAGE 71

. Describing qualities

PRACTICE 1

.: A photographer needs to be patient.

.: He also needs to be artistic.

PRACTICE 2

.: I'm patient and easygoing. But sometimes I'm forgetful.

. Asking about abilities and talents

.: Are you creative?

.: No, I'm not very creative. Are you good at languages?

.: Yes, I'm pretty good at languages.

LISTEN TO THIS   PAGE 73

.: So tell me about your family, Carl.

C: Well, I have one sister and one brother.

.: And what do they do?

C: My sister Rosa teaches ballroom dancing.

.: Really? Does she have her own dance school?

C: No, but she teaches for the biggest school in our town.

A: She must be a very good dancer.

C: Yes, she is. She's also a good singer. She sings in a band when she has free time. And she also has a part-time job teaching German and Russian.

A: That's amazing. She sounds very talented—and busy!

C: Yes, she is always running around doing things. She never stops.

A: Really? And how about your brother?

C: He's a junior at the State University. He's very smart. He's studying engineering.

A: Has he always been a good student?

C: Yeah. He's very good at math and computer science. He loves studying. He's never been interested in sports. Once he starts reading a book, he won't put it down. Sometimes it drives my parents crazy, because when he's studying or reading, he forgets everything else. Sometimes he doesn't even remember to eat lunch!

GIVE IT A TRY   PAGE 75

1. Describing abilities (1)

A: Can you play hockey?

B: No, I can't. Can you?

A: Not very well.

2. Describing abilities (2)

A: What musical instument can you play?

B: I can play the piano. What languages can you speak?

A: I can speak Chinese and English.

LISTEN TO THIS   PAGE 76

M: Wow, Sonia. You're borrowing a lot of books for the weekend.

S: Well, I love reading. And there are some great books in this library.

M: Yes, there are. I see you have some books in Spanish. Your Spanish must be pretty good.

S: It is, I guess. I can speak and read it fluently.

M: Wow. And do you know any other languages?

S: Well, French, but my French isn't very good. How about you?

M: I speak a little German and I'm studying Korean this year.

S: Interesting.

M: Yeah, but I'm just a beginner in both languages.

S: And I see you're borrowing some music CDs.

M: Yeah. I play guitar, and I want to listen to some good guitar music. I teach guitar as well.

S: Really? Are you good at any other instruments?

M: Not really. Just guitar. How about you?

S: I play piano pretty well and I'm learning violin this year. It's fun but I'm finding it really difficult.

M: What other plans do you have for the weekend?

S: Well, I'm going to play some tennis. I'm playing in a tournament on Sunday.

M: Is that right? Is your tennis good?

S: I guess so. Do you play tennis?

M: I do, but not very well. My best sport is baseball. Do you play any other sports?

S: Not really.

Review Unit 7

LISTEN TO THIS   PAGE 78

A: So how was your vacation, Ken?

K: Oh, pretty good thanks. I bought a lot of postcards. Would you like to see them?

A: Hmm. Maybe next time. How was the hotel?

K: It was fantastic. Very comfortable and very good service.

A: That's good. And was the weather good?

K: Not all of the time. It rained a few days, so it was a bit disappointing. But there were some nice days as well.

A: And did you have a good flight back?

K: Oh, it was horrible! The plane was full and the food was terrible.

Review Unit 8

LISTEN TO THIS   PAGE 78

J: So what do you feel like eating?

S: I'm not sure. Any suggestions?

J: What do you feel like? Are you hungry?

S: Yes, I'm pretty hungry.

J: Well, Jenny's Kitchen has sandwiches and hot dogs.

S: What's their food like?

J: It's pretty cheap. I guess it's average. It's not the best place around here actually.

S: Hmm. Any place better you know?

J: Well, would you like to have noodles? Bob's Cafe has noodles and they also serve sushi. I was there last week and their food is terrific.

S: Umm, I don't really feel like noodles or sushi.

J: Boy, you are hard to please. Oh, I know another place. Do you know The Snack Shack?

S: No. What do they have there?

J: They have great pizza!

S: Pizza sounds good to me.

J: OK. Let's go there.

Review Unit 9

LISTEN TO THIS   PAGE 79

C: Well, I've met two possible roommates, and now I have to decide who I like better.

T: Well, Cassy, let's start with you first. What are you like? That will help you to figure out who you'll get along with better.

C: Well, I think I'm easy to get along with. Don't you?

T: Well, yes, you're easygoing most of the time. You're also very reliable—always there when somebody needs you. And you're very neat and well-organized.

C: That's true. I don't like being with people who are sloppy or lazy.

T: OK. So who was the first person you met?

C: Her name is Kavita. She's very neat. Her room in the dormitory is always clean and organized.

T: Right. She's very energetic too, isn't she? She always seems to be working. She never takes any time off. Do you think she's too serious?

C: Well, maybe. But at least I know she's not lazy. And she's very reliable. That's important to me.

T: Now who was the other person? Soon-Ya?

C: That's right. He's very funny. I love his sense of humor.

T: Yeah. He's really creative, too. He's a talented musician, and a good artist as well.

C: You're right. But I don't think he's very neat. His room is always a mess. And he's not so reliable at times. He often forgets appointments.

T: So who do you think your new roommate is going to be?

Unit 10

GIVE IT A TRY   PAGE 81

1. Asking about places
A: Is there a supermarket around here?
B: Yes, there is. It's on the corner of Oak Avenue and Seventh Street.

2. Describing outdoor locations
A: Where's the coffee shop?
B: It's on the corner of Pine Street and 5th Avenue.

LISTEN TO THIS   PAGE 83

A: Excuse me. I'm new in town. Can you tell me a little about the neighborhood?
B: Sure. What do you want to know?
A: Well, first of all, I'm looking for a bookstore. Is there one around here?
B: Hmm. Well the nearest one is on Forest Drive, across from the bank.
A: Forest Drive?
B: Yeah. The bookstore is between 2nd and 3rd. But it's not very good I'm afraid.
A: OK. I'll look anyway. And how about places to eat? Can you recommend a good Indian restaurant?
B: There's one on the corner of 2nd and Pine Street—the Taj Mahal. I go there all the time. It's across from the subway entrance.
A: On the corner of Second and Pine? OK. Got that. What about if I just want coffee?

B: You could try the coffee shop on Grove Street, across from the park. It's across from the gym I go to. It has great coffee and cakes, and the prices are very good.
A: So, the coffee shop is on Fourth and Grove—across from the gym?
B: That's right.
A: How about a hairdresser? I need to get my hair cut.
B: Try the one on the corner of Grove and 2nd. It's OK.
A: Great. And how about a Chinese restaurant?
B: There's a great one on Fourth, next to the gym. But it's very small and it's always crowded.

GIVE IT A TRY   PAGE 85

1. Giving directions
PRACTICE 1
A: Excuse me. Is there a drugstore around here?
B: Yes, there is. Go up Pine Street to the intersection. Turn left at the corner. It's on Main Street, across from the post office.
A: Thank you.
B: No problem.

PRACTICE 2
A: How do I get to the bus stop?
B: OK. Go along Pine Street to the corner of Oak. Turn right onto Oak and walk two blocks. You can't miss it.

LISTEN TO THIS   PAGE 86

A: You look lost. Can I help you?
B: Well, yes, I'm new in town, and I'm looking for somewhere to eat. Where is the nearest cafe?
A: Let me see. OK. So we're on Union. Just walk up Webb Street until you come to Naples Street. Then take a right. There's a cafe on your left. It's really nice. I often have lunch there.
B: Great. And what about a drugstore?
A: Oh, that's easy. Turn left and go down Union until you come to Pine. Then turn right and go up Pine for two blocks. There's a drugstore on the right, on the corner of Green and Pine. I've been there a few times. Their prices are good.
B: OK. And how about a music store? I want to look at CDs and DVDs.
A: Sure. You need to go up Webb Street for about three blocks and take a right at Naples. Go down Naples for a couple of blocks and there's a music store on your right. I hear it's good, but I've never been there.
B: Fantastic. Just one more thing. I hope you don't mind?
A: Not at all.
B: Thanks. These shoes are killing me. How can I get to a good shoe store?

A: Easy. Go down Union for two blocks and then turn right on Pine and go another block or so. There's a shoe store on the corner of Virginia and Pine. I bought these shoes there and they're very comfortable.
A: Thanks so much. And there is just one more question. I want to go to a good club tonight.
B: Hmm. I think there's one near here, but I've never been to it. Yes. Go up Webb for two blocks and turn right on Green. There's a club on your right, on the corner of Scott and Green.
A: Great. Thanks a lot!

Unit 11

GIVE IT A TRY   PAGE 89

1. Asking to borrow things
PRACTICE 1
A: Can I borrow your digital camera?
B: Sure. No problem. Can you lend me your dictionary?
A: All right.

PRACTICE 2
A: Do you think I could borrow your book?
B: Yes, of course.

2. Declining requests and giving a reason
PRACTICE 1
A: Can I borrow your pen?
B: Sorry, but I'm using it.

PRACTICE 2
A: Do you think I could borrow your laptop?
B: Sorry, I need it myself.

LISTEN TO THIS   PAGE 91

1
A: Oh, that looks nice. Is it new?
B: Yes, it is. It's the latest model.
A: It has a nice big screen.
B: Yes, it does. But it's very light. It only weighs 3 kilos.
A: Wow. You know, I'm working on an assignment and I wonder if I could borrow it just for tonight?
B: Umm, actually I will be using it tonight. I have to finish my assignment as well.

2
A: What are you listening to? Music?
B: Actually I'm listening to a Chinese lesson. I'm taking Chinese this semester and we have a test coming up.
A: Oh, I see. Then I suppose you won't be able to lend it to me for the weekend? I'm going away for the weekend and I want to be able to listen to some music on the train.
B: Well, maybe some other time.

This one is nice. It's very light.
: Yeah, I love using it. I play much better with it, and I can hit the ball much harder.
: I'd love to try it some time. Do you think I could borrow it on Saturday afternoon? I'm playing with my cousin.
: Sure, no problem.

: That looks nice. Is it easy to use?
: Very easy. And it takes great pictures. You can download them and put them onto your laptop as well.
: I see. I'm thinking of buying one. Can I borrow yours for a few days to see how easy it is to use?
: Well, actually I'm using it for the next few days.
: Oh, OK. No problem.

: Do you use this often?
: Yes, when the weather is good I ride to school on it.
: How about on the weekend? Do you use it much then?
: Not really.
: Well, do you think I could borrow it on Saturday afternoon?
: Sure. Just come by and pick it up after lunch.

.: I haven't read that. Is it good?
: Yes, it's terrific.
: Can I borrow it when you're finished with it?
: Sure. I'm nearly finished with it. I'll let you have it tomorrow.
.: Thanks a lot.

. **Asking for and giving permission**
: Is it OK if I invite my friends over next week?
: Sure. No problem.

Declining permission and giving a reason
: Do you mind if I watch TV?
: Well, maybe later if you don't mind.

.: I thought I would listen to the sports. Can I turn it on? Is that OK with you?
: Umm, you know, I've got a bit of a headache and I'm trying to rest. Would you mind listening to it later?
.: Not at all. Can I get you something for your headache—maybe some aspirin and some tea with lemon?
: That would be nice, thanks.

2
A: I really feel like a cup of coffee. Can I use the coffeemaker?
B: Do you know how to use it?
A: I think so.
B: All right. Actually I think I'll have one, too.
A: Do you like it with milk and sugar?
B: Yes, thank you.

3
A: Oh gosh, I forgot to call home. I said I would call about now. Is that OK with you?
B: Of course. You can make your call from the phone in the kitchen. It's nice and quiet there.
A: Thanks so much.

4
A: Do you mind if I watch the news? I want to find out what's happening at home and I haven't had a chance to read the newspaper today.
B: Not at all. I'll just turn off the radio.
A: Thanks. I only want to catch the headlines.

5
A: I need to get some clothes ready for the weekend. Is it OK if I use the iron for a while?
B: Yes, it's in kitchen. Look in the cupboard on the left.
A: OK. I see it. Thanks.

Unit 12

1. Talking about past experiences (1)
A: Did you have a good year?
B: It was pretty good, thanks.
A: Did you do anything interesting?
B: Yes, I took a judo class. Did you do anything interesting?
A: No, not really.

2. Talking about past experiences (2)
A: Did you do anything special?
B: Yes. I got a new job. And you? What was your best experience?
A: My trip to the US—I went to San Francisco for a week.
B: Oh, that sounds great!

1
A: Did you have a good year, Taylor?
B: Very good, thanks. Look at this.
A: An engagement ring. Fantastic! I didn't know you were engaged.
B: Yes, I got engaged last month. I met my fiancé when I was on vacation last summer. We're planning to get married next year.
A: Congratulations! That's wonderful news.

2
A: How was school this year, Pei-ling?
B: Oh, so-so.
A: Only so-so? How come?
B: Yes, you know I am very interested in languages, and this year I decided to try to learn German. So I took a German class at night school.
A: Was it difficult?
B: Difficult and very boring. So I dropped it after one month.

3
A: So are you still living near school, Carlos?
B: No, we had to move. So now we're staying out near the airport.
A: Oh. So what's it like out there?
B: Not very nice actually. We hear a lot of aircraft noise, and it takes a long time to get into town.
A: That's too bad. I hate getting stuck in traffic.
B: Tell me about it!

4
A: How was your year, Devi? Did you enjoy your classes at City College?
B: Actually, I didn't complete the year there. I was taking a computer course but I decided I wanted to study business instead, so I changed to a new school— New World Business College.
A: Really? I don't know that school. How was it?
B: Very good. I learned a lot.

5
A: So did you have a good year, Fadi?
B: Not bad, thanks. The best thing was my trip last summer.
A: Where did you go?
B: Thailand and Vietnam.
A: Did you enjoy it?
B: Yeah, it was great.

6
A: Did you have an interesting year, Chloe?
B: I guess it was interesting. But not what I expected.
A: Really?
B: Yeah, I bought a new car.
A: Well, that sounds interesting.
B: Not really. I only had it for a month and someone stole it.
A: No way! That's terrible!

1. Talking about future plans
A: What are you going to do next year?
B: I'm going to get a job.
A: Why?
B: I need to make some money. What are you going to do?
A: I'm going to go on vacation.

2. Talking about wants

PRACTICE 1

A: What do you want to do?
B: Well, I want to get a job.
A: Do you want to travel?
B: Yes, I do! What about you?

PRACTICE 2

A: What place do you want to visit sometime?
B: I want to visit South Africa.

LISTEN TO THIS   PAGE 102

A: So, what are your plans for next year, Robert? And are you still planning to learn Spanish?
R: Maybe not. I think I might try Portuguese instead.
A: Why Portuguese?
R: I'm thinking of going to South America toward the end of the year. I'd like to live in Brazil for a couple of years.
A: Are you just going to travel around Brazil and take a long vacation?
R: I can't afford to do that. I want to get a job in a school there and teach English for a couple of years. I need to save some money to pay off my school loan.
A: Wow! That sounds interesting.
R: I also want to take a photography class.
A: A photography class?
R: Yes. Before I go to Brazil I want to take a class. Then when I'm in Brazil, maybe I can take photos for travel magazines. I hear you can make pretty good money that way.
A: Well, it sounds like you're going to have a busy year. Good luck!
R: Thanks.

Review Unit 10

LISTEN TO THIS   PAGE 104

1

A: Where can I find a supermarket?
B: Go up Ford Street to the first corner and turn right onto Wilson Street. It's the second building on your right.
A: Thanks.

2

A: I'm looking for a mailbox. Is there one around here?
B: Yes, there's one just down the street on the corner of Ford and Wilson. It's next to the drugstore.

3

A: I'm looking for a coffee shop. Do you know a good one around here?
B: Sure. Go up Ford for a block and turn left. There's one about halfway down the first block, across from the bank.

4

A: Where's the subway entrance, please?
B: Oh, go up Ford to the first corner and turn right. There's one on the other side of the road, across from the supermarket.

5

A: I need to see a dentist. Do you know where I can find one?
B: A dentist. Let me see. Oh yes, there's one on Wilson Street. Go down Ford and turn left onto Wilson. There's one about a block down on the left-hand side, across from the hotel.

6

A: Where can I buy some good magazines?
B: There's a very good bookstore not far from here. It's on Wilson. Turn right at the corner of Wilson and Ford. There's one on the corner, across from the bank.

Review Unit 11

LISTEN TO THIS   PAGE 104

1

A: Oh, there's a great TV program on in a few minutes. Do you mind if I turn on the TV?
B: Well actually, I'm trying to study for a test.
A: Oh, never mind.

2

A: It's awfully hot in here. Can I open the window?
B: It is hot. Yeah, please do.
A: Thanks.

3

A: Do you mind lending me this book? I'd like to read it. I hear it's really good.
B: Yeah, help yourself.
A: Thanks.

4

A: Can I use your car tonight? I have a date.
B: Umm, actually I need it myself tonight. I have a date, too.
A: Oh, too bad.

Review Unit 12

LISTEN TO THIS   PAGE 105

A: What are you going to do next summer, Jo?
J: I'm going to go to Australia.
A: Australia. Wow! What are you going to do there?
J: I'm going to travel and I'm also going to work a little to help pay for the trip.
A: Really? What kind of work are you going to do?
J: Oh, anything I can find. Maybe picking fruit or working in a cafe.

A: Great. Are you going to travel with a friend?
J: No, I'm going on my own. But I'm sure will meet people there.
A: Where are you going to stay?
J: I'm going to stay in hostels.
A: That sounds good. And how long are you going to be away?
J: For about six months.
A: Terrific. I wish I could go with you!